'If there is to be a future for the gospel in the 21st century, we need to experiment now with ways of offering the gospel as good news to our culture. The cell movement is an outstanding example of such and deserves our closest attention.'

— *Martin Kennedy*

'Pope John Paul told us we are at a moment of history where God's work is so challenging that there is no place for idleness; the cells are a school of the commitment and the generosity which are demanded by that challenge.'

— ✠ *Donal Murray, Bishop of Limerick*

'This book is an excellent introduction to a creative way of living the gospel as a community.'

— *Breda O'Brien*

'I have experienced the Holy Spirit powerfully at work in the cell system of parish renewal. I am confident that this book will encourage others to adopt the same.'

— *Martin Tierney*

TRANSFORMING YOUR PARISH

Michael Hurley

Transforming your Parish

BUILDING A FAITH COMMUNITY

the columba press

First published in 1998 by
the columba press
55a Spruce Avenue, Stillorgan Industrial Park
Blackrock, Co Dublin

Cover by Bill Bolger
Origination by The Columba Press
Printed in Ireland by Colour Books Ltd, Dublin

ISBN 1 85607 226 6

A booklet, entitled *Transforming your Life,* for use by participants in the *Come and See* course is available from the publishers.

Contents

List of Abbreviations   6

Introduction   7

PART I: COME AND SEE

1   A New Beginning   13

2   Hosting *Come and See*   25

THE COURSE: COME AND SEE

First Meeting   Faith in a Time of Change   37

Second Meeting   Oikos Evangelisation   43

Third Meeting   My Own Story: What I Can Give   50

Fourth Meeting   Revisiting Our Baptism   56

Fifth Meeting   Small Groups:
                    Nursery of Evangelisation   70

Follow-up   78

PART II: CELL GROUPS

3   Introducing Cell Groups   81

4   What is a Cell Group about?   85

5   The Inspiration for Cell Groups   94

6   The Fruit of the Cell Experience   101

7   Questions and Answers   105

Bibliography   123

List of Abbreviations

AA   *Apostolicam Actuositatem* (Vatican II Decree on the Apostolate of Lay People)

LG   *Lumen Gentium* (Vatican II Dogmatic Constitution on the Church)

CL   *Christifideles Laici* (The Vocation and the Mission of the Lay Faithful in the Church and in the World, Pope John Paul II, 1988)

RM   *Redemptoris Missio* (The Permanent Validity of the Church's Missionary Mandate, Pope John Paul II, 1990)

EN   *Evangelii Nuntiandi* (Evangelization in the Modern World, Pope Paul IV, 1975)

Introduction

The course presented in this book, *Come and See*, is a simple five-meeting programme for use in parishes. Where we have used it, it has had such an impact on the majority of the participants that they have wanted more. The 'more' has developed into the growth of small faith-sharing groups in the parish known as cell groups.

This book comes in two parts. The first part introduces, explains and offers practical help in running *Come and See* in your parish. The second part looks at the meaning, purpose and dynamics of cell groups as a means of parish renewal.

I suggest that you read this book right through before deciding on organising *Come and See*. This will ensure that you have a clear idea of the thinking behind and strategies of the cell groups, and it will give you a much clearer overview of the entire project.

A companion booklet, *Transforming your Life*, is published along with this book, for the use of participants in the course.

Pope John Paul II sees the present moment in history as of immense significance. He calls upon the entire church to commit all of its energies in proclaiming Christ. Every believer must take up this supreme duty. He often refers to the need for a new evangelisation. When speaking of Western Europe he tends to speak of a re-evangelisation. This is to say that he sees Europe as having largely lost contact with its Christian roots. It has again become missionary territory. Indeed it is claimed that Western Europe is the most difficult territory of all for the evangelist, providing the greater challenge in the proclamation of the gospel:

> 'I sense that the moment has come to commit all of the church's energies to a new evangelisation and to the mission *ad gentes*. No believer in Christ, no institution of the church can avoid the supreme duty: to proclaim Christ to all peoples' (RM, 3).

His challenge is for all. Within these pages a story is told, the story of the impact of a course upon individuals. As a result they began to journey together in faith-sharing groups. It is about the questions raised. It is about the quality of relationships. It is a story about a community placing evangelisation on its agenda and where mission is understood as one's presence amid the interaction of daily relationships.

The course may be perceived as very formal and very structured. That is the inherent risk in seeking to put it on paper. In practice, as I have experienced it, this perception is very far from the truth. It has meant many happy and funny moments, with some very good friendships formed and deepened. It has always been a great joy to observe someone opening their life to the sunshine of God's love and coming to a new decision to Christ and to the church.

This series of meetings is obviously not to be followed slavishly. Much of what is presented here is given by way of guideline and resource. It works when the leader and the core team wish to use this material to communicate, not words, but a living faith. It can be adapted to suit very differing backgrounds. A number of diverse parishes and groups have used it and given us very positive feedback. You can expect to be surprised by God's goodness as you see people growing into a community of people, and taking a new interest in, and responsibility for, the gift of faith and for the mission of the church.

Come and See is aimed primarily at those who are not very involved in the life of the church. It is intended for the ordinary person in a parish, who may no longer be very sure as to the basics and foundations of their faith. People who have lapsed and who wish to give the church another chance have found it a complete new beginning. Those who had been very committed found in it a great renewal of faith and a vision as to their place in the service of God.

What you will see is very much a community event, which has seen the involvement of many during the last seven years. I am indebted to the parish cell system at Ballinteer. Simply to witness the readiness of so many to take on a deeper commitment was truly inspirational for me. Their openness, honesty, and living faith became for me missionary territory as we shared together, seeking to interpret life in terms of God's love and to let faith make a difference in the culture around us. Their happy community life became for me a parable, teaching me of the holiness and commitment by which lay people wish to live and of their giftedness as they seek to serve God and those around them.

I extend a special dedication to Ethel Byrne, Hilary McCann and Noel Ryan for the trust they placed in me and for becoming companions with me from the beginning in what was for each of us a pioneering into a gradually unfolding future. I thank too the executive members, leaders and cell members for their love, advice and prayer.

We referred many issues and difficulties to Fr Mike Eivers during our early days. I thank him for his patience and wise comments. I owe him a great debt of gratitude. Fr Martin Tierney was always available to us. I thank him for his judgement, and for communicating to us an inspiration and an enthusiasm to continue on the path we had chosen.

St Eustorgio, Milan, where Dom Pigi Perini is parish priest, was special to us and gave us a sense of what is pos-

sible. We sought the advice and guidance of Bishop Donal
Murray, our area bishop, and of Canon Séan Carey, our
parish priest. I thank both of them for their encouragement. I still remember Bishop Donal's advice. He told us
that if we looked only at the possible difficulties, we
would never start anything. We thank them both for all
their help to us. I am indebted too to Fr Eamann Cahill,
Patricia Mitchell, and Fr Des Forristal, for their encouragement and advice.

Bishop Dermot O'Mahony has always been a great
friend and support to me. He has helped me at a number
of defining moments in my life. I owe a deep gratitude to
him.

I thank Archbishop Desmond Connell for the trust he
placed in us, and for assuring us that what we were doing
was making another contribution to the church.

I thank my own family who shared their faith with me.

I have changed the names of some people from whom I
quote, in order to protect their anonymity.

Finally my deepest gratitude to Seán O Boyle of Columba
Press who made this production possible. I thank him for
his interest in this series of presentations, and for his advice and wise comments.

This work emerged because so many people believed during the last seven years that 'a further shore is reachable',
that our rich tradition still speaks to us. They were prepared to set sail for a distant shore, expressing a living
faith seeking to speak to and enrich contemporary culture.
In giving they received. They found a deeper faith, a belonging to a community and above all a mission.

My hope now for you is that you too may find a new ur-
gency in taking up the mission of the church and that as
you give, you will be enriched and blessed.

PART I

Come and See

CHAPTER 1

A New Beginning

I was appointed as junior curate to the parish of St John the Evangelist, Ballinteer in 1986. It was a relatively new parish, constituted in June 1974. I suppose it was true to say that the first phase of its life was coming to an end, namely the dedicated work of plant building, with emphasis on raising finances to meet the costs. A great spirit had been generated through the various fund-raising ventures. Much work too had been directed to the parish as a faith community. I think especially of the Ministers of the Eucharist and the programme by Wim Saris, which was a religious programme aimed at harnessing in a united effort the work of home, school and parish.

A question that soon came to the surface for me was: what *is* a Christian community? And a second one followed: how does one build a community, whose foundation and inspiration will be faith? These questions had two sources: firstly, what people were saying to me about the need for adult religious education and of their concern that faith be part of the lives of their teenagers and children; and, secondly, my own observation that people were very busy with work, family and some parish activities. For many the quality of their commitment to faith was very strong. But it did not translate into a *community* way of life. Indeed the element of isolation struck me as being very real, where people living in a neighbourhood did not know those a few doors away. Was this because people were too busy? Did it reflect a middle-class mentality that sees faith as private and having little to do with the way people relate to one another? It was possibly a combination of all these factors and many more.

During my first years I heard all types of aspirations and hopes for the parish expressed by parishioners. The provision of bingo for the elderly rated highly. I was, however, continually drawn to the relationship of faith and community.

We hosted quite a number of prayer events, directed retreats and talks in response to requests. We also sought to explore the thinking of those who wished that faith would speak to everyday living. Together with two leaders of the prayer group and a few others, I decided to attempt to put together a series of talks and discussions which would be aimed at the busy parishioner. That was in 1990 and we ran it as a series during Lent.

Our hope was to create a climate where people would share faith with one another. We sought advice from many people. We drew on our own experiences and upon what we had seen work, like participation in a covenant community for me, marriage encounter for a few, and upon the skills learned in the workplace. We drew largely from the Life in the Spirit Seminars, used by Charismatic Renewal. This is a basic course in Christian initiation to bring people to conversion to Christ. Our emphasis was not just to provide information on basic themes, but more importantly to offer inspiration within a prayer setting, where people would get to know each other and form some community links.

We then gave much thought to the presentation of each night and in particular to those who would give the teachings. We set our dates and invited a variety of well-known speakers as we wanted people to witness different approaches and emphases. We also looked for variety in presentation: the first two nights were talks, the third was the personal stories of young adults, the fifth was a homily at

Mass. We booked a school classroom which would comfortably seat up to forty.

We had no idea how parishioners might respond. We had accepted that thirty might attend. Our next task was to nominate and meet with those who would act as guides or leaders in the small groups of four or five participants. We looked for a number of qualities: that they be people of integrity, that they have compassionate and understanding hearts, that faith be important to them and influence the way they live, that they possess skills in relating to others, that they be teachable, and that they be ordinary parishioners seeking to have some degree of order in their lives. We also wanted a male and female balance. We needed eight to ten, we reckoned. We were reluctant to invite those who were seen to be 'involved in everything'. They were already busy. We were also eager to involve at least two people who were not involved in parish life to offset the perception that it is always the same people who are involved in everything. Those already active were, with some gentle persuasion, largely positive towards the idea of serving as guides. We found it more difficult to nominate and to encourage those not already involved. We received a number of negatives responses. They felt unprepared for what we were asking of them. Eventually two agreed to act as guides.

We met the prospective guides about two weeks prior to the course. We outlined its purpose, summarised the talks and explained clearly what we expected of each. We emphasised that they were not there as experts, but rather to care for and encourage those in the small group. They were present to ensure that people made personal responses to the questions given, to recognise 'tangents' and to create a climate where each person would offer their own thoughts. They would invite each person to remember to pray daily for one another. They were to see themselves as also participating in the group by simply and briefly sharing their own personal response to the questions while facilitating others to do likewise. The purpose of the small group was explained as giving people time to appropriate what they had heard and to express something of their personal faith. In this way they would learn from one another. This meeting ended with a time of prayer for the course and for one another. They were to meet again one hour before the beginning of the course for prayer and to become familiar with the theme, content, speaker, questions and format of the night.

We met the guides for a half an hour after each night's presentation. This was to review what had happened, to hear any questions that may have arisen for them, to keep basic principles before them, like drawing people back to what is personal in the groups, and to share a brief prayer of gratitude to God. The theme of the next night was given, with the reminder to meet together an hour beforehand.

Three weeks prior to the event, we began to look at who our audience might be. We saw it in terms of two primary sources. Firstly, we pitched it at the ordinary busy person in the pews. We put together an attractive brochure containing the theme of the course, the heading of each night and the names and descriptions of the speakers. It also carried a tear-off slip which each could return with the course contribution. We gave a lot of thought to the question of money. We finally judged that naming an amount was correct. It defrayed our expenses, but more importantly it would communicate a seriousness about the course. It would less likely be seen as 'dogoodery' on our part. The entire approach and wording of the brochure was directed at the person who might never have attended anything of a religious formation nature but who might want something more from their faith. We had a three-week advertising campaign. There were announcements in the parish, inserts in the newsletter, posters in the church porch and in a few local gathering places. The brochures were left available at the church exits. The Sunday prior to the course, we got a number of people to hand brochures to people as they left the church. There was also a facility for booking in, as well as making further enquiries, at an office set up in a room at the rear of the church during the morning. We invited the prayer of those attending the morning and evening daily Masses.

Secondly, we started to share with our friends and our various contacts throughout the parish something about the course, inviting them to participate. This proved to be very successful, with well over half of those who eventually attended having been personally contacted. It showed us the value of a one-to-one invitation. It was what we were later to know as the working out of *oikos* evangelisation. Mary was one of the people I invited. She was to arrive, much to my surprise, with her husband, Joe. He explains: 'I had been involved in many community activities over the years. I was thinking of doing something different, like attending a course in the local college. I saw the brochure. I knew that my faith was not very good. Why not give it a go, I thought, at least for the first night? To my surprise, it was the boost I needed. It made us aware of a religious aspect in our relationship.'

We arranged to have a folder for each participant, which included blank paper, pen, music sheet, brochure, an article on the understanding of parish as a community of disciples, a 'road map' with various hazards depicting the road of life, asking the question: Where are you? It was a simple gesture, but it gave the idea of preparation and a little professionalism.

In the meantime we had approached two guitarists to prepare a music sheet and to lead us in song as part of our worship of God. The hymns to be selected were to include some traditional ones, with others being simple and 'catchy', which would convey a sense of being gathered together in praise of God. They would include a few reflective ones. All should be easy to sing. The two guitarists sought a few others to join them as singers. They met on a number of occasions to rehearse, but especially to pray the hymns together and to enter into the spirit of each. Their task each night was to be a simple one, namely to lead with two or three hymns at the beginning, to draw the time of scripture reflection to a close with a hymn and then to end the night by leading everyone in another one or two. But they were to make an invaluable contribution, as they drew people into an expression of faith that was joyful and bonding. All joined in the singing. It was different from the somewhat rigid style that they associated with Sunday worship.

Replies were slow in coming back to us. We wondered if we were on the right track. We ran the risk of being greatly embarrassed, with very highly acclaimed speakers committed and a possible attendance of only ten to fifteen people. Disappearing fast were our plans to have assigned individuals to small groups, with a guide appointed for each. The opening night was fast approaching. Names were coming in. We were now happier; at least there would be twenty-five.

We nominated a welcoming team of three. Two would be seated behind a table. One was to hand out folders and name tags to those who had already returned the brochure with the fee. The other was to take the names of those who decided to attend on the night, and to accept contributions and present folders. It was a pleasant surprise when we saw that she was the busy one. Forty-six people attended. The third person remained in the vicinity of the entrance welcoming people, allaying any apprehensions and directing them towards the room.

The core team and guides had already emerged from their meeting. They began offering a friendly greeting and a helping hand to all, hoping that their own nervousness was not being picked up.

It was with a great air of expectation that people gathered. We had a pleasant difficulty before we began. Forty-six arrived. We needed extra chairs. In our planning we had people nicely arranged in two concentric circles. Now it became a question of placing a chair in every available space. It was interesting watching the variety of those arriving. A few were coming on their own, but most were accompanied. They were nearly all middle aged. Quite a few married couples arrived. We observed that a number of 'certainties' to attend, who were present at every religious event, did not come this time around. There were also some 'real surprises'. There came a few whom we would have considered being more at home in the local pub or on the sideline of a football pitch exhorting their team to greater endeavours. They came too from almost every part of the parish. Everyone who came on the first night attended each following night, except where there were prior commitments. This was to our surprise and to our great encouragement.

We had given much attention to the layout, lighting and presentation of the room. We provided a blackboard as well as an easel and charts. Nearby we placed a lectern, with a banner and slogan draped down the front. We had a small low table covered with a white cloth. On it lay a large candle and a small white cushion, where the scriptures would later be placed. Two large bunches of flowers were placed in containers at the front of the table. On the wall behind the speakers was a large banner with a slogan summarising the theme of the night.

Guitars had been tuned. A 'Hello' from one of the music group indicated that we were ready to begin. Much of the opening hymn was muted behind the chatter of seeming surprise as people greeted others they recognised. A second hymn was sung. A friendly welcome and explanation was followed by a prayer. The taking and placing of the scriptures on the cushion was accompanied by a prayer of enthronement. Then the passage assigned was read twice. We waited for a response, but only one came and this was from one of the team. But we were on our way. We could see that people were beginning to relax. They enjoyed the night. All were to return.

The first night was rather quiet and reflective, with people enjoying the experience, especially the opportunity to share and chat within the small group. The night on story telling was somewhat different, and on looking back, central to the fruitfulness of the course. It was a night when we invited a number of young adults from the parish to share their personal faith stories. They taught one of their hymns, which included gestures, and also presented the theme of conversion through the medium of a short sketch. Here were young people talking about their faith in God and relating to him as friend and as person. This was new for many present. Faith was to a great extent intellectual and God was at a distance. It all made them review their own relationship with God and encouraged them to know their own faith story. Moreover, the fact that these were young people meant that they presented a challenge without it causing a great threat. People were able to see it as an invitation to a personal faith, while at the same time seeing it as the expression of youth who were taking their faith seriously.

Another key night was the celebration of the Eucharist. I led it, and I began with the premise that deep resentments, hurtful traumas and sin can obstruct us from experiencing the goodness of God. I drew greatly from the ceremony of baptism to highlight the richness of the sacrament. It also communicated an assurance that this 'new thing' that they were now experiencing was in fact rooted in the church. At the time of prayer, each person came forward. I invited married couples to come forward together. My prayer for them included the accepting of the grace that is theirs from their sacrament of marriage. During this time the music group sang gentle hymns, while everyone remained in a spirit of prayer for one another. The night ended with each person being presented with a lighted candle, and we all sang together 'This Little Light of Mine' and 'The Light of Christ'.

Each night began promptly on time and ended exactly ninety minutes later. This night was the only exception. It lasted for about two hours. People had been informed at the end of the previous night that it would be much longer and were given a brief outline of what to expect. No questions were raised. Indeed the feedback indicated that this was a special event. They appreciated rather than resented the extra time. Many declared that they were aware of making an adult commitment to Christ, that they had experienced a deepening of faith and a great sense of gratitude to God for his goodness. Many also said that, as they joined together in prayer towards the end, they wanted to go home and share the good news of what had happened to them.

Listening to the feedback during the final night and to the informal comments of many, it became quite evident that the participants wished this experience to continue. Our response was to invite them to a further night when we would explore the options of follow-up. We approached this with a certain bias. We were clear that we did not possess the necessary information and capacity to provide teachings and talks from our own resources. We were also aware that there is a limit to the availability of guest speakers. Neither had we any finances available to us. It had also been our experience from similar attempts at adult religious education in the past that many would cease to participate after some time. We knew we would be very fortunate were the group to settle down at fifteen or so.

We put together a format for the night similar to the previous ones, with prayer, scripture, etc. The theme of the teaching was the reality and formation of Christian community and the place of small groups within it. In the feedback, it became obvious that there was a great interest in the possibility of meeting in small groups. A number of obvious questions surfaced: How to select homes for meetings? How to choose leaders? How to train and support them in a new ministry? How to decide who goes to which home? How to co-ordinate these groups so that they would not become just isolated groups within the parish? What programme(s) to be followed? How to communicate the emphasis that these groups will always look outwards towards the church and world rather than inwards upon themselves and upon their own difficulties?

A decision, with almost unanimous agreement, was taken to begin meeting in homes and to trust that we would learn as we proceeded. Cell groups had come into existence, even though it was about a month later that we described them as such. We called them 'home groups'. Twenty-eight were to attend the first meetings. They were hosted and directed by four couples in four different districts within the parish. The opening of homes was a courageous step in a parish which was relatively new and where people did not greatly interact with one another.

The first few meetings in the homes brought their own difficulties. Niall and Pauline explain: 'When it came to the time of the singing we closed tightly the windows and doors. We pulled the blinds. We sang with muted voice. We did not wish to be seen or heard by the neighbours. This lasted only for two meetings. We spoke with a few neighbours and explained the meetings. We assured them that they would always be welcome. We began to consider it a privilege to have prayer in the home.'

So much fitted into place so naturally that we now recognise, in the course and in the direction of the follow-up, a providential moment for us. We accept it as grace, as God's goodness to us. Should you want further information of the birth and support of the cell groups at this initial stage, the Ballinteer Cell Community or the National Co-ordinating Body will be very happy to be of service to you.

The original course has been reviewed after each time we hosted it. This has meant many changes. Each time we have seen it bear fruit for each of the participants. The biggest change in *Come and See* has been its reduction from seven to five nights. It substantially retains its original format, together with its emphasis on personal conversion, on the church as community, and on inspiring a spirit of evangelisation. Should you consider taking up this course and using it according to your situation and needs, we are confident that, with God's blessing and with good leaders who operate out of a living faith, it will equally bear much fruit for you.

In conclusion, I share a thought with you which carries a reflection that has been inspirational for us, and has encouraged us in sensitive times. It is the story of Gideon, which can be read in Judges, chapters 6 and 7. Israel had been under siege by the Midianites for seven years. Gideon was furtively toiling away at his winepress when he heard the voice of the Lord, 'Yahweh is with you, valiant warrior' (6:12). This caused a great degree of resistance within Gideon; indeed, he became quiet negative. Yahweh could not be with him. In fact he must have deserted him. Gone were the good old days when he was able to see the great deeds of God, especially when he brought his people out of Egypt. So he wished not to get involved.

Yahweh again turned to him: 'Go in the strength now upholding you, and you will rescue Israel from the power of Midian. Do I not send you myself?' (6:14). Gideon still had other ideas. He protested that he was the weakest member of the weakest tribe in all Israel. Yet Yahweh had chosen Gideon. Finally the message began to sink in for

Gideon. He began to prepare and to gather a huge army around him. But this was not Yahweh's idea. He wanted him to go with only three hundred. All those who were frightened and fearful were sent home, as well as those who were not prepared to undertake humble tasks.

The task was ridiculously immense. The enemy were so many that the valley was 'as thick as locusts. Their camels were innumerable like the sand of the seashore' (7:12). God accomplished his plan through Gideon and his insignificant followers so that Israel might not claim that they achieved success through their own might and strength.

There were many times when we stood in Gideon's shoes. Today we are thankful that we did launch into the unknown with little resources and at times with little confidence in our own abilities. People don't need another programme. What they do need is an 'anam-chara', a 'soul-mate', a faith friend, or a few people who will walk the journey of life with them. They look for someone to believe in them. They too need a spirituality, a way of interpreting life and relating to God which engages them personally. They wish to experience that God is part of all the ups and downs, joys and disappointments of their lives and that they in turn can, through his grace, hold a candle of hope for others.

My hope for *Come and See* is that it will not just be a programme put on for others, but an introduction to a deeper spirituality, and that each participant will find an 'anam-chara' as they begin a journey with others in community.

CHAPTER 2

Hosting *Come and See*

In this section I will offer some simple thoughts which may help you to host this series. I will do so on the assumption that this is your first venture. It will take on its own life for you, and you should adapt what you read here to suit your own circumstances.

When?
At any time of the year – Advent and Lent being especially suitable.

Where?
In a private room, in a hall or in a church.

For how many?
Suitable for a small group of about ten, or for a large gathering.

For whom?
Anyone who wishes to experience a more living faith.

Checklist of requirements:
- Develop a clear reason of why you wish to host the course.
- Agree on times and a location for course.
- Select a core group to take overall responsibility.˙
- Get people to pray for its success.
- Invite speakers, giving them a clear brief.
- Choose and train guides.

- Appoint a music leader to form a music group. Select hymns for the music sheet.
- Decide on ways to advertise – brochure, newsletter, church notices, etc. Consider a two-minute explanation at Sunday Masses.
- Agree on where application forms, with contributions, are to be handed in.
- Consider the ambience of room – lighting, banner(s), table, flowers, seating arrangements, podium.
- Appoint a hospitality team, and arrange for welcoming newcomers.
- Plan folders for each participant.
- Make this book available for sale and give each participant a copy of the booklet, *Transforming your Life*.

Clear Reason:

This is your starting point. Your purpose for hosting this course is most important. It is not sufficient that it be the 'putting on' of another activity. The purpose for this course, I believe, needs to run deeper. You may have wished, for some time, to initiate a process to help people share their faith with others. You may have wished to explore faith as it relates to everyday events and relationships. Here you have a resource to do so. If you genuinely believe that small groups are beneficial in a parish community, then you have here an ideal opportunity in working towards them. This course ideally begins with a sense that one is being called to help others discover a more living faith, who will then take a greater responsibility in encouraging others to do likewise. It is a call to contribute towards building a faith community.

Time and Location:

The duration of each meeting is 1 hour 30 minutes. It is important that meetings begin punctually and end on time. They can be run at any time, when people are available to meet. The numbers available will determine the location. Where there is a small group of eight to twelve, it may be hosted in the informal atmosphere of someone's home. This has an advantage in that it can prove to be a 'trial' run, before launching it with a wider audience. Alternatively, some of those participating can repeat the process with others in their own homes.

The flexibility of the course is such that it can equally be effective for big numbers in a local hall or church. We have seen it work best when there have been between 35 and 50 attending.

In treating of the other headings below, I will be assuming an effort aimed at a large gathering, even though much of what is outlined will also have significance to home meetings.

An ideal time to host it with a large group is during Lent and Advent. People may be more receptive to a course of this nature during those times.

Core Group:
While there will be an overall leader, it is important that it not be seen as his/her idea and project. Others will relate more openly where they see a team of people working together and eager to serve one another. They will catch a faith atmosphere when they witness a team at home with the singing, the sharing of scripture and the spontaneous prayer. They will more readily look outwards towards others when they see people eager to listen to them and to ensure that this be a good experience for them.

This leads to the importance of a core team. It should number between three and seven. In some situations such a team may easily be selected. In others it may prove far more difficult. A number of pointers may help.

• Those selected should have an ability to work together. This does not mean that they be already close friends, which may indeed only give the impression that the core group is a clique.

- Aware of those who hold influence within the parish, it is important that the core be to some extent representative in terms of social class, districts, education, spiritualities, involvement, etc. For example, it is best when there are those who have previously been active within the parish as well as those who have not.
- Those who form the core need to be striving to live with integrity and honesty, while clearly realising that they have not arrived. A judgmental attitude of knowing all the answers for themselves and for others can be counter productive.
- Each needs to be teachable, possessing a readiness to learn new insights and new procedures. They are to have pioneering attitudes, launching into the unknown with confidence and even excitement.
- They need to share to some degree an appreciation of their Catholic identity and of the richness of their tradition.
- It is good to seek a diversity of giftedness within the core. One may be good at presentation, another at secretarial work, another at administration, another at leading prayer, etc.
- Above all, each is to share some sense that they are being called to undertake this course so that others may find a deeper faith within a faith community.

Team formation will take more or less time depending upon the experience of those selected. Where people have already a familiarity with sharing faith with others, the need to spend time together will not be great. It will mean a few meetings to clarify the purpose of the course, to discuss its content and its practicalities, and to agree in a general way what may be expected as a follow-up. It may simply be agreed that it be an event of five weeks' duration, which will enrich participants in their personal lives. Prayer together, reflection on a scripture passage, a few hymns and petitioning God's help and wisdom must be part of their time together on every occasion. Tasks will be assigned for one or more meetings of the course during their final meeting together, e.g. to lead a prayer, to read the scripture, to facilitate the feedback.

Formation takes much more time where sharing prayer and faith are alien to those on the core team. It will be more important here to place emphasis upon building a faith community among them, as this will be a new experience. This can be done simply by joining together in a hymn or two at the beginning, by reading and sharing in a personal way upon a scripture passage, and ending with a time of intercessory prayer. It may be necessary to take six or seven meetings together. Such meetings will also include communicating in a simple way a vision of parish as a community where people share faith with one another. They will also outline the course content and its practicalities

It is possible to minimise meetings during of the course. The core team, with guides and speaker, can meet about 45 minutes prior to each scheduled opening time, for prayer together and to become familiar with the presentation and questions of the night. A brief time of review can take place at the end, for fifteen minutes when the participants have departed. It makes for a long time together, but it eliminates an extra meeting. It works.

Prayer:

Prayer is essential to the success of this course. Faith is a gift of God. It is the mysterious interaction of the individual with God. We can only create a climate where this gift is accepted and celebrated. We cannot create faith. Hence this course is approached in prayer, expectant that God will use it to draw all participating into a deeper realisation of his love for them. The core team commit themselves to a time of daily personal prayer. The prayer of others is invited. In one parish in Belfast, a prepared prayer was recited at every public Mass for three weeks prior to, and during, the course. In another instance the prayer of a nearby contemplative order was invited. Each participant is also encouraged to set aside fifteen minutes for personal prayer each day.

Speakers:

The choice of speakers needs to be made well in advance to give time for preparation, but especially to ensure their availability. It is good to look for a variety of presentations. The meetings call for different approaches. The opening meeting is a talk. It calls for an understanding of social, cultural and religious change and indicates how each person can be a pioneer at a time of transition. When this is given by a visiting speaker, it has the advantage that those taking part will more readily see that the course is not parochial. They will know that others too are seeking a living faith in today's world. The third is best in story form. It is given by one who is in touch with their own faith story. Try for balance of male/female and local/visiting speakers. Speakers are selected on the basis of what best serves the group, and they should have conviction, an ability to communicate, and a living faith.

Guides:

The task of a guide will be to facilitate the small group discussions. The criterion of selection is similar to that for the core team. Again guides need to be representative of the parish community. They may include those on the core team. They will lead small groups of four to five. They invite each member to make a personal response to the questions asked. It is very easy for a guide to dominate in the group as others look to him/her for answers. This is to be resisted. They are to respond personally and briefly to the questions. Others take their cue from them when it is their turn to speak. It is important to be alert to tangents, to what takes the group away from personal responses. A good catch-phrase is 'Keep it personal'. The guides are alert to encourage those who may be shy in speaking. They will also ensure that no one person dominates and will attempt to involve everyone equally . It can be difficult for people to express sentiments of faith within a group when it is new to them. What they expect from the guide is simply to know that they are heard and understood. Great reverence is to be extended towards those who speak of their personal faith. The guide needs to have an appreciation of the place of silence. Where there may be no words, people can still remain present to one another. They need time to reflect quietly. Initially, there is the temptation to fill up every silence with words. The guide encourages those silences which are filled with presence, of God and of one another.

As the course progresses, the guides should ensure that a prayer is said when the small group comes together and again at the end before feedback in the larger grouping. The task of a guide is a happy one. It may be compared to that of a mid-wife, who encourages new birth. It is so inspirational to witness another struggle to a deeper sense of God's providential love. The guide prays for each one during the course of the week. S/he is attentive to the needs of each and will be available should there be need of a one-to-one conversation.

The training of guides need not take a lot of time. One or two meetings should be sufficient. It includes clearly outlining the task involved, the pitfalls to be watched, the purpose of the course and a time of prayer together. They are not selected to be experts. They are simply to help others to appropriate personally the teaching presented.

Music:

It is best to give the task of selecting the music to one per-

son, who then can get the help of others, try to arrange for
a musical instrument, provide a hymn sheet or book, and
lead the singing at each meeting. There is a vast selection
of new hymns today. It is also wise to include a few which
are a long time in use but continue to have meaning for
many. Hymns are sung at the beginning, often after the
scripture reflection, and to draw people back from the
small groups. One or two hymns conclude the meeting
(often the 'Our Father').

Advertising:

Those who will attend will largely do so from a personal
invitation. People will more readily participate when they
know of others who will be doing so. The core team and all
involved in preparation carry the responsibility of telling
their friends and neighbours, who may in turn inform others.
Some will also attend because of a public announcement
or reading a poster.

Advertising is an area that deserves much planning. It
is a witnessing to faith. There is not much value in having
good news when no one knows about it. It is a task that
one person undertakes, with the active assistance of all. In
every community there are creative individuals who can
formulate attractive ways of communicating a future
event. It is best to understand advertising as the preparation of the parish. It attempts to notify all of an important
event. It can also raise consciousness of the need for a continuing formation in the faith. Ideally it should invite the
prayer and support of all for a new venture.

The usual channels are the church notices, posters for
porches and public places, local radio, newspapers and
fliers. I know of one area where people distributed fliers at
the local shopping mall and spoke with those who passed
by. In many places a two-minute presentation was made at
all Sunday Masses two weeks previously. Each area will
draw up its own plans and time frame.

There needs to be a direct effort to attract those who sit in the church pews on a Sunday or less often, but who are otherwise distant from the parish and from any religious involvement. The course is aimed primarily at them. It has lead to a deepening of faith for those who have greater commitment. It has prompted a conversion for a number who had been alienated from the church. The emphasis, however, should be an appeal to those who are busy and who may not see themselves as religious but who may now wish to give some more attention to faith. One parish put together an attractive brochure. One section was headed: 'Who is it For?' It explained:

1. For anyone who wishes to take their Catholic faith a little more seriously than just Sunday Mass
2. For the lonely person who does not have friends.
3. For the person who does not have faith but who is searching for something.
4. For the happy person who wishes to give something of themselves to others.
5. For the one for whom the bible is a closed book and is seeking help.
6. For the one who is seeking calm and quiet.
7. For the one who wishes to join in building a parish community.
8. For the busy person.

Return of forms:

Many may wish to book for the course beforehand. It needs to be clearly stated on all advertising material where and when the forms will be accepted.

Booking in:

It is good to set aside a table, with cloth and a few chairs, near to the entrance. It will be staffed by one or more who will present each person on arrival with a folder and a name tag. They will check off the names of those who had previously booked and take the names of others. They may also assign people to the small groups.

Ambience of the room:

A room communicates. We normally simply think of a place of meeting, without referring to its language. It is important that the atmosphere be suitably lighted, airy, without being uncomfortably hot or cold, and colourful. Making available a podium, a table with cloth, a few banners, a flipchart, gentle music as people enter, flowers and proper seating arrangements can make such a difference.

Hospitality team:

The core team nominates a few people whose task is to greet those arriving who may be quite apprehensive and uncertain, especially at their first meeting. They will warmly welcome them. They will try to answer any questions asked. They will chat to them as they usher them to their seats. They may introduce them to others who may be from the same street or district. They should have their names on display so that they can be called by their Christian names. This will allay some fears. More importantly, it builds a spirit of community, where people know they are welcomed and served. It communicates a happy atmosphere.

Folders:

Making folders available, with participants' names, has two advantages. It shows preparation on the part of the core team and implies that they are taking this series of talks seriously. It also puts together material that will be of benefit to those taking part. It will include a pen, paper or note book to write upon, a hymn sheet, the flier advertising the course so that the topics and names of speakers are seen, and the participants' booklet. A core team may also insert other material, like a letter of welcome, a brief history of the parish, an article from a magazine which outlines a vision of parish or one which will be helpful in personal prayer and reading of scripture, a story of someone's faith journey, some item of fun, or a caricature. Folders are easily put together. They make such a difference.

Sale of the book:

The participants' booklet, *Transforming your Life*, should be made available to each participant. Copies of this book, *Transforming your Parish*, might also be made available for sale. It gives a fuller understanding of the background and content of the course and may provoke thought about what is possible for individuals and for their parish. It will also be beneficial to make available a limited number of the Veritas video, *A New Vision of Parish Renewal*, which deals with the importance and place of small groups.

The participants' booklet:

Transforming your Life contains three items which will be of help to the participants. Firstly, it gives some background to the course and what they might expect at it. Secondly, it gives an outline for the clarifying and formulation of one's faith story, which arises in meeting three. And thirdly, and most importantly, it gives, in a section called *Living Words*, scripture quotations and reflections for use on each day of the course. This is to assist each person to a deeper prayer and to the use of scripture.

Conclusion:

Our simple hope in putting this course together is that it may be of some help to you. Our prayer is that it will lead to a gathering of disciples within your community, to raising an awareness of the importance of each individual, to the beginnings of a community of communities within your parish, where people will seek opportunities to share their faith with one another and with all whom they meet.

Launching into something new, which you suspect has immense possibilities, is exciting and also daunting. It is important to realise that only God gives the growth. We need not feel burdened. I borrow an attitude from the fifteenth-century mystic, Julian of Norwich in her book *Revelations of Divine Love:* 'We are God's bliss. He endlessly delights in us ... I saw three longings in God. The first is that he longs to teach us to know him, and to love him always more and more, as is suitable and profitable to us. The second is that he longs to bring us into his bliss ... The third is to fill us with bliss ... to last forever ... The greatest honour we can give to Almighty God is to live gladly because of the knowledge of his love'.

My greatest joy has been to journey with others in a common mission. My greatest 'bliss' has been to hear of their prayer, support and love for me during those times when I expressed my uncertainty and inferiority before them. Such has been my experience when we first undertook the course presented here. It was a journey into the unknown with much questioning and self-doubt. It never ceases to inspire us to hear how God uses this course to lead others to him and to a faith community.

Each journey beings with a single step. The destination may appear far away in the distance. We will certainly never arrive without setting out. As Karl Rahner says: 'In the torment of the insufficiency of everything attainable, we come to understand that here, in this life, all symphonies remain unfinished.' You are beginning an exciting journey with others. We will be delighted to hear from you and to offer you our limited resources.

Faith in a Time of Change

Sing a hymn or two to draw people together into a sense of God's presence.

Welcome all the participants
It is important to be friendly, easy and natural in manner and in style. Some people are excellent at speaking about the difference that the course has made for them in a humorous, and yet honest way. They may be equally good at identifying and allaying the apprehensions that many people will have on their first night. They may bring a fear of what it might involve for them when faith and prayer are public, nervousness at meeting new people, and suspicion that they may be with religious freaks.

Outline the aims and objectives of the 5 meetings of the course:
Aim: To help people speak about their faith with family and friends.

Objectives:
Week 1:
To appreciate the changes in today's world which call for a new response in faith, and to see where hope is found at a time of transition.
Week 2:
To know of the daily opportunities to let your faith speak.
Week 3
To know what you should say when you wish to share faith with others.

Week 4

To decide to take a greater responsibility for your faith.

Week 5

To find out what will best support you to live a life of faith.

Aim of the first meeting:

To appreciate the changes in today's world which call for a new response in faith, and to see where hope is found at a time of transition.

Objectives:

To know of the profound changes that are taking place in the world and in the church today.

To see the relevance of God's Spirit to every age and culture.

To come to the One, Jesus, who brings life out of apparent death.

To become a pioneer in speaking to our contemporary culture.

Opening Prayer: We begin with the following or a similar prayer:

God, our Father, we thank you for each person here. We come, aware that each of us is unique and that we come with a wisdom born out of all the experiences of our lives. We come too with our own sense of inadequacy, with our many unanswered questions, and with a need to love and be loved.

God, our Father, we seek your wisdom that the gift of faith be renewed for each of us. We thank you for your Son, Jesus, who makes all things new. We thank you for the gift of your Spirit who continues to renew the face of the earth.

We ask you for your blessing upon this course. We

seek your blessing for each of us during these weeks.
We make this prayer through Christ, Our Lord.
Amen.'

Scripture:
We listen to the Word of God, which is from John 11:32-44.
*It is good to give a place of prominence to the scriptures at the
very beginning by placing them, for example, upon a cushion on
a table with a lighted candle. A simple prayer and/or ceremony
may accompany such a beginning. The scriptures will occupy, as
a point of focus, the same place each night.*

A time of silence is observed after the reading.

John 11:32-44 is again proclaimed.

*People are now encouraged to share a word, a phrase, or a
thought from the scriptures that draws their attention. Have a
few people read the passage in advance and be willing now to
share simply and briefly. They share to encourage others to do so.
Normally people are reluctant to speak at the first meeting, but
such sharing will grow during the course.*

Teaching:
A speaker is introduced. A member of the organising
team, a parish staff member or an invited guest gives a
teaching. A different speaker may be selected for each
meeting. A teaching in this setting has greatest impact
when it is between eight and fifteen minutes in length.

People identify best with the speaker when s/he includes some personal content. The following will help as a
useful guideline:

1. We tend to take for granted what is most familiar
to us, like the air we breathe, the ground we walk
upon. Faith is part of who we are. We have grown up
with it and can easily take it for granted. We can then
often experience a sense of inadequacy when we are

asked to discuss or explain some central aspect of our faith.

2. It is a time of profound transition in society. It is a long way from the horse and trap, in which I remember travelling to Mass as a child, to present-day space travel. Give an example that you observe. Many people today feel that they exist upon sifting sands. Changes in the church and different emphases are also often perceived by people as adding to the sense that 'all is flux', and that all is changing. Give one or two examples of the changes that you see.

3. Bishop Donal Murray in his Lenten Pastoral, 1997, stressing the need to live the gospel at this time of rapid advancement in technology and communications had this to say: 'We are the pioneers who have to discover how Christ speaks to the contemporary world and how we can be his messengers to it.'

4. Many people too experience a loss of morale, largely due to public issues in which the church is embroiled and to the negative way in which the church is perceived by so many.

5. God's Spirit is ever active and ever relevant to people, with their complex questionings and hopes.

How then does our faith speak to the realities of today?

Where is our anchor to live in a secure way?

Where do we look for pointers and direction to live with confidence and a sense of mission?

Personal references here will be very appreciated and leave deep impressions.

6. There was a clear picture in the scripture reading. It was of Jesus standing outside the tomb, the place of darkness and of death. He says 'unbind him and

let him go free'. We too can imagine Jesus standing outside the tomb of our very selves. He wants us to identify what the tomb may mean for us. Where are we dead? Where are we in darkness, not being at home with ourselves and with other people? Where are we bound by having little hope and meaning in life? Might we not be tempted to react like Mary, thinking that the crisis is because Jesus is absent? What causes us deepest sadness as we look at the church and the world to-day?

Maybe there is a pattern of life here. Things have to die before new life can emerge. Could it be that what is really happening in society and in the church is that so much that we have clung to is dying and that amid the seeming confusion and chaos are the possibilities of new life? It is for us then to know the signs of the times, the movement of God's Spirit, the mind of Christ, as he looks with love upon the world he has created. It is for us to discern how we can be co-operators in his mission in the world. It is for us to know his Spirit, who blows where he wills and is relevant to every age.

From our tomb, from our place of uncertainty and even confusion, we can await his voice as he speaks: 'Unbind him/her and let him/her go free' and hear his voice offering new life to us and to the world.

Observe a time of silence.

Questions:

These questions are best dealt with in groups of three or four participants with a facilitator. Always keep bringing people back to personal responses.

1. Indicate a change in society and one in the church that you observe. How do you feel about these changes and how do you respond to them?

2. Where do you find guidelines for your life in this time of rapid change?

Feedback: Each group briefly reports what came up for them from the questions asked.

Notices:
(a) A summary is made of this first meeting. The presenter may briefly refer to a change that s/he has seen and offer a reflection on being called to witness within the community. A brief reference is made to the next meeting – who the speaker will be and the topic to be explored.
(b) People are encouraged to take some time each day for quiet and reflection. A word of explanation is given as to how this time can be most fruitfully spent and how to make best use of the 'Living Words', which are scripture references with a reflection, included in the participants' booklet as a help to prayer.

Aim of next week's meeting:
To know of the daily opportunities to let your faith speak.

Final Prayer:
God our Father, we thank you for to-night, for all that we shared, for the different ways we interacted, for all the encouragement given and received. May these nights be a new beginning for us. May you now nurture and bring to fruition the good work you have begun in us through Christ, Our Lord. Amen.

Sing a hymn to conclude the evening.

Oikos Evangelisation

Sing a hymn or two to communicate a sense of the presence of God and to encourage people to turn to him in praise, offering him their concerns, their hopes, and their fears.

Welcome all the participants

Aim of last week's meeting:
To appreciate the changes in today's world which call for a new response in faith, and to see where hope is found at a time of transition.

Aim of tonight's second meeting:
To know of the daily opportunities to let your faith speak.

Objectives:
To see evangelisation as a primary thrust for people of faith.

To provide a vision for each person to engage in the work of evangelisation in a way that fits into their normal activity and relationships.

Opening Prayer: We begin with the following or a similar prayer:

God our Father, we thank you for all those who, through their words and example, have inspired us to know and to follow you. We thank you for our parents, who brought us to the baptismal font. They were eager that we should grow up knowing the story of Jesus. We thank you for the many times they mentioned your name to us.

We thank you for our teachers, our priests and sisters, and for all who sought to pass on faith to us.

We now ask you to again fan into a flame the gift of faith that in many ways has been dormant within us. We desire to be your people, who will not be afraid to speak of you in our homes, our places of work, and in our schools.

God, our Father, we seek your continuing blessing upon us as we make our prayers through Christ, our Lord. Amen.

Scripture:

John 1:35-46 is proclaimed. After a time of silence it is again read. People are then invited to share one-to- one (in twos) some insight or thought which the scripture provoked for them. Three or four people may then declare in public their thoughts on the scriptures read.

Teaching:

The following thoughts are intended as guidelines and resources for the speaker:

1. *Oikos* is the Greek word for household or a house of people. It is used many times in the New Testament. It is used in Acts 10:24: Cornelius 'had called together his relatives and close friends' (*oikos*), when Peter came to him. Your *oikos* is the network of

people whom you relate to on a regular basis – family, friends, neighbours, those at work and at school. *Oikos* evangelisation refers to the quality of those relationships It sees your daily network as the most effective place of ministry. Reaching out through channels of relationship is God's natural means of witness, by means of personal example and the spoken word. *Oikos* evangelisation, then, is a very rich concept. It means loving those we meet each day. This includes serving, listening to deepest needs, praying for, sharing your values and faith with the purpose of leading them to delighting in God's love for them.

2. It is estimated by the AA that each alcoholic affects for the worst at least eight people in a significant way. It must equally be true that each person can affect at least the same number towards taking a step to a deeper faith and trust in the Lord and towards living a vibrant life of witness and worship in the church.

3. We have got it wrong. *Get the right priest ... Have a mission ...* In various studies in the States it is estimated that about 85% of those who return to the church and to a deeper faith do so at the invitation of a friend or a family member.

Do we reach out with our faith? Or is it something private and not to be shared?

Yet what do we do with a good news story? Do we not relate it with our friends? Is faith then not a gift to be given away?

Frank Duff: 'I have to repeat my sad little definition, that a Catholic is one who is unprepared to help others in points of faith' (1956).

Evangelii Nuntiandi (Pope Paul VI, 1976): 'We wish to affirm once more that the essential mission of the church is to evangelise all people. Evangelisation is the special grace and vocation of the church. It is her essential function. The church exists to preach the gospel.'

Redemptoris Missio (Pope John Paul II, 1991): 'The evangelising activity of the Christian community is the clearest sign of a mature faith. The effectiveness of the church's organisations, movements, parishes, and apostolic works must be measured in the light of this missionary imperative. Only by becoming missionary will the Christian community be able to overcome its internal divisions and tensions, and re-discover its unity and its strength of faith.'

Matthew 28:18-20: 'All authority in heaven and on earth has been given to me. Go, therefore, make disciples of all the nations; baptise them in the name of the Father and of the Son and of the Holy Spirit, and teach them to observe all the commands I gave you. And know that I am with you always; yes, to the end of time.'

4. How well are we doing at our primary duty? Not great, we must admit. That is not to make anyone feel guilty. Many people are very concerned about passing on faith – parents to their children and teachers to their class – but overall we are doing badly. We are running a great secret organisation and keeping the good news under cover from the world.

When did you last share your faith, your personal story of your trust in God, with another? You are not alone. Only about 2% of people have a true missionary spirit, of really wanting others to know about Christ, and seeking opportunities to speak about him.

Go out to the whole world: We live in a network of rela-tionships of home, school, work, leisure, neighbourhood. We are called to bring the spirit of the gospel to bear on these relationships. It is estimated that we meet about twenty people each day.

We must be ready to share the hope that is within us. Vatican II says that we must be ever ready to put into words our faith, for believer and unbeliever alike. Most important is the example of our lives.

In Ballinteer, in Dublin, up to 300 at one time met, in groups of four to twelve, to ask what was the impact of their faith on the world around them. It was a time of prayer, of reflection on a scripture passage, but especially a time of review of how well they were sharing their faith. These groups are a place of sharing difficulties, and of encouraging one another by telling about what works. They are a place of support. They are where one gets in touch with one's faith story and grows in confidence to share it.

5. *George Bernard Shaw:* 'I am of the opinion that my life belongs to the community, and as long as I live, it is my privilege to do for it whatever I can. I want to be thoroughly used up when I die, for the harder I work the more I live. Life is no "brief candle" for me. It is a sort of splendid torch which I have got hold of for a moment, and I want to make it burn as brightly as possible before handing it on to future generations.'

We may suspect that we have little to give. But life is no 'brief candle'. We can shape the world we live in. We have daily opportunities to influence others and to encourage them to draw closer to God. You may never see the work of your life. It may be many years before it comes to fruition.

Observe a time of silence.

Questions:

These questions are best dealt with in groups of three or four participants with a facilitator. Always keep bringing people back to personal responses.

1. Discuss the idea of *Oikos*.

2. Speak in general terms about the difficulties you have experienced or are likely to experience in sharing your faith with those of your *oikos*.

Feedback: Each group briefly reports what came up for them from the questions asked.

For the coming week:

1. Explain the value in writing down the names of those with whom we interact on a regular basis. This is one's *oikos*. Such a list can be a reminder of our 'missionary territory'. It can serve as a review of how well or badly we relate with the people we meet with regularly. It can be an occasion to thank God for each person we meet and for the unique gift that each brings. Encourage each person to undertake this exercise during the coming week. It is purely for one's own benefit and will not be needed for the next meeting. It is intended to give clarity to one's loving.

2. Encourage each to take a time of prayer during the coming week. Invite them to ask the Lord for his wisdom to discern what is the deepest need of each of them so that they may love them as he loves them.

3. Encourage each to share some aspect of their personal faith or of something that they find helpful in living with hope. This they may do with at least one person on their list during the week. It would be appropriate to tell them what the course already means to them at a personal level.

Conclusion:

The presenter thanks people for attending. S/he refers to

the 'Living Words' as a help in prayer. In one or two sentences he summarises this meeting. This may take the form of briefly telling how an understanding of, and a focus on, *Oikos* deepened his/her attention to life' relationships.

Aim of next week's meeting:
To know what you should say when you wish to share faith with others.

Final Prayer:

God our Father, we thank you for each person who has ever influenced us to be who we are today. We thank you for their love for us. We thank you for those who shared their faith in you. It led us to a deeper trust in you and inspired us to a greater service of all whom we meet. We thank you for the special people who, as we look back, stand out for us as people of great vision and love and who have inspired us. We pray for our parents, our teachers, our priests and sisters and for all who have helped us.

We thank you for our families and for those we meet each day. We pray for the gift of love that we may love them as you love them. We pray that, through your grace, we can, by our love, by our example and by our words, lead them to you. We especially present to you any one of them whom we are aware of who needs your love in a special way at this time. We ask you to bless and to protect each of us during the coming week.

We make our prayer through Christ, our Lord. Amen.

Sing a hymn to conclude the evening.

My Own Story:
What I Can Give

Sing two or three hymns to help bond people together as a community and to direct their thoughts in worship to God.

Welcome all the participants:
The leader refers to the previous night and enquires how the week has gone for everyone.

Aim of last week's meeting:
To know of the daily opportunities to let your faith speak.

Aim of tonight's third meeting:
To know what you should say when you wish to share faith with others.

Objectives:
To get in touch with, and to know one's own unique faith story and to recognise in it the grace of God in one's life.

To write one's faith story.

To know that one's story is a gift for others.

Opening Prayer: We begin with the following or a similar prayer:

God our Father, we thank you for our time together. We thank you for this time in our lives when we know we can turn to you in total trust and confidence.

God our Father, we thank you for each moment in our lives. We thank you for our parents who gave us the fragile gift of life. We thank you for the time when we were brought for baptism. We then became in a special way a child of yours and part of your people. We thank you for our confirmation, that special moment when we were anointed for service, empowered to be a witness for you. You then called us to speak for you before others.

We each thank you for the moments and events of life until this day. There were moments of great joy and also moments of great sadness. There were moments when we knew your presence in a very caring and personal way. There were moments too when we thought you were absent.

We now take some time in silence, inviting your Holy Spirit to walk with each of us back through our life to recall a moment of special grace and significance.

After a time of silence, we conclude:

We make this prayer through Christ , our Lord. Amen.

Scripture:

We listen to God's Word, which tonight is taken from John 20:19-31. After a time of silence it is read again. People are now invited to share briefly what the scripture may have prompted for them.

Teaching:

The following provides useful guidelines, when used with personal examples by the speaker: The preferred way to present this teaching is to do it briefly and then invite another to share their personal faith story or to get one or two young adults to do so.

1. 'The people of our day are more impressed by witness than by teachers, and if they listen to these it is because they also bear witness' (*EN*, 41). People today are tired of words and of the interpretation of words, and are more interested in the personal lives and experiences of others.

2. I have often heard stories by people on radio and television. The values they expressed were not mine, yet there could be no denying the personal experience of another. This is also true of an authentic Christian story when someone speaks about the moments they found a new and richer faith or about how they experienced God as helping them through some difficult times. We are always deeply impressed by statements of conviction.

3. The fact is that each of us has a story to tell, indeed we have many to relate. It is often said that each person has at least one good book that s/he could write. Such is the richness of each of us. Such is the richness of God's action in our lives. To unpack our stories we invite the Lord to travel back through the events of our lives and look again at the significance of a few of them for us today, in particular as each may have deepened, or otherwise, our relationship with God.

4. Many books already carry various methods to help us review our life's journey and to see God's grace and goodness to us. The simplest help I have come across is to present to each participant paper and a pen. Ask each to draw a line across the entire page. That line now represents one's life from birth to the present moment. Mark off sections, each representing ten-year periods. As they look back over

their lives each will be able to recall significant moments, like First Communion, the birth of their child,
the death of someone they loved, which God used to
draw them closer to him. People who were a significant
influence will also be recalled. It is important to see
why they were so significant. Their being present to
us at a critical time for us? The words they spoke to
us? The fact that we knew they loved us? Their obvious commitment to God? The example of their lives?

Follow-up
Give people a few minutes to mark off and name a number of spe-
cial times when they realised God was close and very real for
them. They are also to name people who greatly influenced them
towards a deeper and richer relationship with God. A large blank
sheet of paper, with a pen or pencil, had been made available so
that each may draw a line representing their life and on it mark
in important dates.

In groups of three or four, participants share what they are
comfortable with about the special times and people that they
have recalled.

A time of feedback is beneficial in deepening a sense of God's
action in one's personal history and of clarifying the qualities
that made people influential in one's life.

Summary and Conclusion:
(a) In our scripture reading to-night we saw a defining moment for Thomas. He exclaimed 'My Lord,
and my God'. He would be different. Here was a big
grace for him which would always be part of him
and to which he would often refer. He had a new
story to tell.
The disciples too had a new story to tell: 'We have
seen the Lord'. They had heard his voice. They were
to be different. They were leaving behind some of
their old fear and were entering into a greater joy
and confidence in the Lord.

(b) You too have a story to tell. As you have looked
back you have seen the Lord in different moments
and events. That's your story. That's your message
and good news for others to hear. You have looked
too at the people whom God has used to influence
and shape your story. You can continue to learn from
them how you too can be used by God to be significant in the lives of those who cross your path in life.

(c) Display and explain *My Good News Story* from the
participants' booklet. It is intended to be of benefit
towards knowing your faith story. It is important
that each person write out their story to clarify it for
themselves and to become more at home with. They
then 'will always have your answer ready for people
who ask you the reason for the hope that you have'.
(1 Pet 1:15). Each is encouraged to write out their
story during the coming week and to be open to
share it with someone in a sensitive and caring way
should an opportunity present itself. They will not
be asked to read it at the next meeting.

(d) Encourage people to take fifteen minutes or more
in quiet reflection with the scriptures during the
coming week.

(e) The format of the next night's meeting is explained. We will be revisiting our baptism to experience the new relationships to God, to oneself and to
the community that it communicates, and also to
offer ourselves in commitment to living those relationships. Mention whether there will be a celebration of the eucharist or a service of prayer.

(f) People may welcome the Sacrament of Recon-
ciliation as a preparation to giving their lives to
Christ, availing of this healing and forgiving moment. Give the times when it is available locally.

Aim of next week's meeting:
To decide to take a greater responsibility for your faith.

Final Prayer:

> God our Father, we thank you for the fragile gift of life. We thank you that in your goodness you called us into life. We thank you for your Son, Jesus. We thank you for his constant presence in our lives. We thank you that he has walked each step of our journey of life with us. We thank you that we can see the mystery of his action and love in our lives.
> 'If I asked darkness to cover me,
> and light to become night around me,
> that darkness would not be dark to you,
> night would be as light as day.
> It was you who created my inmost self,
> and put me together in my mothers womb;
> for all these mysteries I thank you:
> for the wonder of myself, for the wonder of your works.
> You know me through and through,
> from having watched my bones take shape
> when I was being formed in secret,
> knitted together in the limbo of the womb' *(Ps 139)*.

The prayer is concluded after a moment's silence

> We make this prayer in praise and gratitude to the Father, through Christ, our Lord. Amen.

Sing a hymn to conclude the evening.

NB: An alternative way to present the above teaching would be to invite someone to share their own personal story. This has the value that participants will hear at first hand the impact of a good story about Christ's activity in a person's life. It would be important that a time limit of fifteen minutes be set, otherwise there is the danger that a lot of unnecessary details would be spoken about.

Revisiting Our Baptism

Sing a hymn or two to draw people together into a sense of God's presence.

Welcome all the participants

Aim of last week's meeting:
To know what you should say when you wish to share faith with others

Aim of tonight's fourth meeting:
To decide to take a greater responsibility for your faith.

Objectives:

To explore your relationships and life in the sacrament of baptism.

To experience the meaning of baptism, when one is adopted as a child of God.

To make a commitment as an adult to Christ.

To take responsibility for the gift of your faith.

To know you are called to let your light shine

Format of the night:
The format of the night is explained. This night has a special impact upon people when it is in the context of a Mass. It is as if it expresses best the participation of everyone in coming to the Lord as healer, who evokes from each one a wanting to hand their lives over to him, sharing in the of-

fering of Jesus to the Father. However, the format followed below is that of a non-eucharistic celebration, which can easily be adapted.

Opening Prayer: We begin with the following or a similar prayer:

Lord Jesus Christ, we thank you for coming to show us the Father. Lord, we thank you that at our baptism, you came to make your home in each of us. We thank you that at our confirmation you gave us power, through a new gift of your Spirit, to be witnesses to your love and goodness in the world. We thank you for the many moments of your grace that we have known during life.

Lord, tonight each of us comes before you to give our lives to you. We now want to make an decision as adults to follow you. We want to take on a greater responsibility for the gift of faith that has been handed down to us.

We thank you that you have been drawing us to you. As we come to you with openness and honesty, we know that we can expect, through your Spirit, a renewing of our faith and a new experience of what it means to be a child of the Father. And so, Lord, we commit our lives to you, knowing that you wish to do the most loving thing in each of us and to empower us to be your people in the world today. We make our prayer through you as Lord and Saviour. Amen.

Time of Healing and Repentance:
Explanation and background information

The good news is that on average we have a major crisis only every ten years. The bad news is that the crisis lasts about seven years. That's the view of some psychologists. How accurate, it is for you to judge! So the majority of us are living through some stage of a crisis. There is no escaping the cross. Welcome to the club.

How we handle it is important. We can be crushed by it. It can also be the making of us as people. I am sure you know people who have suffered deeply and yet seem contented and wise people. Maybe it was precisely their suffering that made them. They had so many reasons to be bitter but they chose to be better. So how we deal with suffering is most important.

How do we handle a crisis?

1. It is important to talk through issues that arise. We can easily think that here is my cross and it is for me to grin and bear it. So we try to be heroic and keep it all to ourselves. The fact is that when we deal with it in that way it may haunt us at a later date, through our lashing out in anger or by withdrawing into ourselves.

So the first thing is to believe in talking, not to anyone or everyone but to someone you can trust. It may even involve going to some professional or to some supportive group. At times we think this is being disloyal, especially when our difficulties are linked with another. We should not see it that way. It is simply finding help and caring for oneself. We are not good at asking the question: 'What do I want?' We are not good at looking after ourselves.

God works through nature. And if we don't come to terms with some issues, like anger, resentment, fear, and talk them through, it is very difficult to come to know the God who loves us.

2. It is important to realise that we are sinners:
'If we say we have no sin in us, we are deceiving ourselves and refusing to admit the truth; but if we ac-

knowledge our sins, then God who is faithful and just will forgive our sins and purify us from everything that is wrong. To say that we have never sinned is to call God a liar and to show that his word is not in us' *(1 Jn 1:8-10).*

Here St John gives us a basis to speak about sin as both personal and social, and what we are to do to deal with our sinfulness.

3. We need to turn to the Lord for healing and forgiveness: This opens us to the experience of the good news in Jesus Christ. We bring these issues to him in prayer.

So let us pray.

Guided Prayer:

God our Father, you sent your son Jesus, not to condemn the world but that people should experience acceptance, healing and forgiveness. We thank you for the gift of your Son, who makes his home in us through the gift of your Spirit.

Lord Jesus, we thank you for revealing your Father's heart as prodigal and lavish in his love for those who turn to you. We thank you that in your death and resurrection you conquered suffering, sin and death. We now seek the wisdom of your Spirit to walk with each of us through all the events of our lives and to prompt us to stay with any event that needs attention and/or forgiveness.

We turn from all sin. We want to see the horror of our failure to love you and others. We present to you for your forgiving love the times we have deliberately walked away from you and the times we have knowingly damaged others and/or society, through our injustice, through our selfishness, through manipulating the emotions, and even the very personhood, of others. Reveal our deepest sin as we now take a time of silence, awaiting your Spirit to guide us to the real truth of our lives and to areas of repentance.

Lord Jesus, we want to be people of truth. We want to be people who live in the light. We now repent of our sin. We know you are present to us as the one who forgives sin. We turn our lives completely over to you. We accept you as our Lord and Saviour. We thank you for welcoming us into your love and that your forgiveness is real. Your mercy is new each day and we thank you for now clothing us once again as a new creation.

Take some time for people to be alone with their own thoughts. Some may wish to take a few moments visualising the Lord's love for them, seeing his eyes of mercy gazing upon them, or being enfolded in his embrace of them.

A time of silence

Jesus came, too, to heal the wounds of sin and division.

Lord, you have said: 'I have come so that you may have life and have it to the full!' (Jn 10:10). Lord, we ask your Holy Spirit to walk with us to the places of darkness in our lives. We live in a world of sin and division, where people hurt and are hurting. We pray that you take us to an event which has deeply distressed us and which we think still holds us captive.

Lord, I enter into that time of distress. I feel again the sense of being alone, the confusion, the sense of no one being there to help me. I feel again all the emotions that may have surrounded it: – rejection, the guilt of thinking that it was my own fault, the futility of life as I looked into the future. Lord, I stay here for a short time, reliving again this time of darkness.

Lord, I now look to you. That moment is now present to you. I see you walking into that time in my life. What are your eyes of love and compassion telling me?… Your hands reaching out to me: What are my thoughts? … I see your smile, as if you wish to bless me … I hear your whisper: What are your words that you are speaking in my ear?…

Lord I know you can free me from being held captive by the anger, the fear, the inferiority before others and the resentment that is still part of me from that time

Lord, I know that 'by turning everything to their good you co-operate with all those who love you' (Rom 8:28). Lord, I present all the painful situations of my life to you … the addictions … the times of fear … the times I felt betrayed and crushed … I pray that the experience of my weakness and brokenness will lead not to despair but to new trust in your goodness. I pray too that through knowing my own poverty you will lead me to a deeper understanding and compassion towards all who are in need.

Lord I thank you for all my life, for all that I may describe as good and for all that I may describe as bad. It has all led me to this moment, when I give my life to you as the one who heals and forgives. Fill me now with a deep love for you and for all whom I meet each day.

We make our prayer through you, the Christ, the Son of the living God. Amen.

Instead of some of the above there are many prayers for inner healing which you may find useful.

Scripture:
The cure of the man born blind, Jn 9:1-12.

Teaching:
This is to be brief. The following will be a helpful guideline.

1. Imagine the vibrancy of the blind man – his sense of joy, of wonder and of discovery. He was healed of his blindness. He had received what he had been looking for – his sight. We too live with blindness. We don't see God as he is, as 'a devouring fire' of love, which Isaiah describes. We don't see ourselves as we are; as sinner, in need, yet a child of God, totally loved by him. Our dignity is such that he even comes to make his home in us. Thomas Merton, describing his deepest identity, said: 'I am one who is loved by God.' We don't see others as they are. It is often said that were we to stand before a congregation of people and see people as they are, we would need dark glasses to prevent being blinded by the radiance and the light of Christ before us.

Tonight we are about to renew our baptismal promises. We pray that it will be a grace for us, revealing who we are as the children and the family of God, which is our inheritance from our baptism.

2. In the gospel we see the power of Jesus to change, to heal and to make a difference. It is in the name of the same Jesus that we gather. When we lose the sense of the power of Jesus, we lose the power of Christianity. It remains a structure, a legal system, a moral code, but without the expectation of the influence of a living God.

Renewing our promises is to expect the release again of God's Spirit in our lives. The experience of the early church is also for us to-day. 'What you see and hear is the outpouring of the Holy Spirit' (Acts 2:33) is equally for us here and now. The expectancy of faith in the Risen Christ, that made people bring the sick and the infirm and lay them along the side of the street so that the shadow of Peter might fall upon them, is to inspire us to a greater expectancy of faith.

3. The blind man had a part to play. He knew he was blind. He did something about it. He allowed Jesus to draw near. Then he went and washed in the waters at Siloam.

We too have a part to play. The truth, however, is that we may not wish to change. We probably know people who live in intolerable situations, but they fear living in a different way. We too can be afraid to let go of our sin and of our selfishness, because we fear not being able to cope in a new situation.

All that is expected of us is to allow ourselves to be drawn closer to Christ and to trust that he will do the most loving thing in each of our lives. We must give him permission to do in and through us what he wants to do.

4. The man spoke about the difference Jesus made in his life. He told the story exactly about what had happened to him. He is now an evangelist. 'An evangelist is a witness to the experience of Christ' (Pope John Paul II). He has known the power of Christ. He has a story to tell. He has good news to share with others to encourage them to come to the source of good news. Too often our witnessing is ineffective, or shied away from completely, because we have not ourselves known the power of Christ to make a difference. One of the obstacles to evangelisation is 'the apathy and especially the lack of joy and hope in many of our evangelisers' (EN, 79).

Quotes: 'Those who have been evangelised become themselves evangelisers. This is the proof, the test of the genuineness of their own conversion. It is inconceivable that those who have received the word and surrendered themselves to the kingdom should not themselves become witnesses and proclaimers of the truth' (EN, 24).

'The men of our day are more impressed by witness than by teachers, and if they listen to them it is because they also bear witness' (*EN*, 41).

Renewal of Baptismal Promises

Layout:
You need a table, nicely arranged, with white cloth, a few flowers, a large bowl of water, with salt nearby, the paschal candle, a small candle for each person present with a name and a ribbon attached to each. Lighting should be soft.

The ceremony is best led by someone associated with leadership in the parish or the community as a sign that the commitments being made are within, and for the life of, the church.

The actual ceremony of baptism is closely followed, taking account of this particular setting. Through listening to the words we hear again what is ours through our baptism and are awakened to experience it now with an adult decision.

Welcome:
> The Christian community tonight again welcomes you with great joy. In its name you were claimed for Christ our Saviour by the sign of the cross.

Each person makes the sign of the cross on his/her forehead as association with that moment when it was first made by parents and godparents.

Prayer of Exorcism and Anointing:
We take the authority of Christ over all evil.

> Almighty and ever-living God, you sent your only Son into the world to cast out the power of Satan, spirit of evil, to rescue your people from the kingdom of darkness, and bring them into the splendour of your kingdom of light. The prayer at our baptism was for you to set us free from original sin, to make us temples of your glory, and to send your Holy Spirit to dwell within us. We were anointed with the

oil of salvation in the name of Christ our Saviour to strengthen us with his power, who lives and reigns for ever and ever. Amen.

Blessing of Water:

Praise to you, almighty God and Father, for you have created water to cleanse and to give life.

All: Blessed be God

Praise to you, Lord Jesus Christ, the Father's only Son, for you offered yourself on the cross that in the blood and water flowing from your side, and through your death and resurrection, the church might be born.

All: Blessed be God

Praise to you, God the Holy Spirit, for you anointed Christ at his baptism in the waters of Jordan so that we might all be baptised into you.

All: Blessed be God

Come to us, Lord, Father of all, and make holy this water which you have created so that all of us who are renewing our baptismal promises may again be washed clean of sin and be born again to live as your children.

All: Hear us, Lord

Lord, make holy this water which you have created so that we whom you have chosen may be born again by the power of the Holy Spirit, and may take our place among your holy people.

All: Hear us, Lord

Profession of Faith:

You have come here to renew the promises made for you at your baptism. By water and the Holy Spirit you then received the gift of new life from God, who is love.

On your part, you must make it your constant care to continue in the practice of the faith. See that the divine life which God gives you is kept safe from the poison of sin, to grow always stronger in your hearts.

If your faith makes you ready to accept this responsibility, renew now the vows of your baptism. Reject sin; profess your faith in Christ Jesus. This is the faith of the church.

Do you reject Satan?

All: I do

And all his works?

All: I do

And all his empty promises?

All: I do

Do you believe in God, the Father almighty, creator of heaven and earth?

All: I do

Do you believe in Jesus Christ, his only Son, our Lord, who was born of the Virgin Mary, was crucified, died and was buried, rose from the dead, and is now seated at the right hand of the Father?

All: I do

Do you believe in the Holy Spirit, the holy catholic church, the communion of saints, the forgiveness of sins, the resurrection of the body, and life everlasting?

All: I do

This is our faith. This is the faith of the church. We are proud to profess it in Christ Jesus our Lord.

All: Amen.

Procedure:

Participants are seated near to their guide (group leader). Each person in turn comes forward to the blessed water. They pause for a moment in silent prayer and then make the sign of the cross with the water, as a link with, and a commitment to, the reality of their baptism. This is a gesture of their commitment to Christ and of their 'yes' to appropriating their baptism through experiencing being a child of God and a member of his family.

Their guide accompanies each, standing behind them, and placing a hand on their shoulder immediately before they make the sign of the cross. This is a reminder of the support of the community as they now seek to commit themselves to living a more vibrant faith. In the early days of the church this gesture was also part of the prayer of the community for the outpouring of the Holy Spirit on those seeking a deeper faith.

They stand in front of the bowl of water, where they are greeted by the leader. The participant may be asked: 'What do you wish us to pray for?' After the sign of the cross the leader places a hand on the head of the participant. The prayer may be very simple, for example, 'May the Lord meet the desires of your heart.' Where time allows, and when the numbers are small, there may be a longer time of prayer, when the guide, who knows them well from the previous weeks, may also verbalise a prayer for each. A married couple may come forward together and this can also serve as a time of renewal of their marriage.

Meanwhile everyone else is in prayer. They are praying for one another as they observe others move forward, publicly declaring for Christ and renewing their faith commitments. This is normally a time of quiet reflective prayer. Hymns are sung as a backdrop to prayer. During this time, those in the small groups may pray for one another. This has the value that the prayer is personal.

The above procedure can be adapted for a very large gathering by having a leader and blessed water at different places around the hall or church.

After everyone has returned to their places the following,
from the rite of baptism, is said:

God the Father of our Lord Jesus Christ has freed
you from sin, given you a new birth by water and
the Holy Spirit, and welcomed you into his holy
people. At your baptism he anointed you with the
chrism of salvation. As Christ was anointed Priest,
Prophet, and King, so may you live always as a
member of his body sharing everlasting life.

All: Amen

You have become a new creation and have clothed
yourself in Christ. At baptism you were clothed in a
white garment as the outward sign of your Christian
dignity. With your family, friends and the community
to help you by word and example, now continue to
bring that dignity unstained into the everlasting life
of heaven.

All: Amen

(When the Eucharist is celebrated, there now is the presentation
of gifts. The following will then be the rite of dismissal.
Otherwise, we proceed as follows.)

Each person comes forward on hearing their name called out,
announcing: 'N, Receive, the light of Christ'. They come to the
paschal candle, where the candle previously set aside for them is
now lit and presented to each. The following is said when all
have received their candle.

These lights are entrusted to you to be kept burning
brightly. You have been enlightened by Christ. You
are to walk always as a child of the light. May you
keep the flame of faith alive in your hearts. When the
Lord comes, may you go out to meet him with all the
saints in the heavenly kingdom.

The Lord Jesus made the deaf hear and the dumb
speak. May he continue to touch your ears to receive

his word, and your mouth to proclaim his faith, to
the praise and glory of God the Father.

All: Amen

Final Prayer:

By God's gift, through water and the Holy Spirit, we
are reborn to everlasting life. In his goodness, may
he continue to pour out his blessings upon us, who
are his sons and daughters. May he make us wherever
we may be faithful members of his holy people. May
he send his peace upon all who are gathered here in
Christ our Lord.

All: Amen

Sing a suitable hymn or two, e.g. *This Little Light of Mine,
The Light of Christ, Go Tell Everyone.* All are holding their
lighted candles. Their is a great sense of joy and a looking
out to the world to bring the light of Christ.

Notices

Take care in extinguishing the lighted candles.

A reminder that people meet again next week. Refer to the
theme of the meeting, which will look at the way(s) we can
be supported in living out our faith joyfully and with conviction, with particular reference to the support and encouragement a small faith groups can give.

Should you agree on a buffet reception on the final night
advise people to bring something to eat (and to drink).

Thank people for taking extra time tonight and offer a
word of encouragement. They are indeed the Light of
Christ for others.

Aim of the next meeting:

To find out what will best support you to live a life of faith.

Small Groups:
a Nursery of Evangelisation

Sing a hymn or two to draw people together into a sense of God's presence.

Welcome all the participants

Aim of last week's meeting:
To decide to take a greater responsibility for your faith.

Aim of tonight's fifth meeting:
To find out what will best support you to live a life of faith.

Objectives:

To understand the ideal of parish as a community of communities.

To summarise how the church views the place of small groups.

To communicate the importance of small groups to support you in living out your Christian life and to help you to share your faith.

To explain the Ballinteer Cell Experience to help you to catch a vision for your own life and for your parish.

To give an outline of a cell meeting.

Opening Prayer: We begin with the following or a similar prayer:

> God our Father, we thank you for again bringing us together in your name. We thank you for sending your Son, Jesus to form a people. We thank you for the gift of your Spirit, who is at work within us leading us to you, to one another, and to the service of all whom we meet.

> We thank you for our time together. We thank you for the gift of one another. We thank you for the ways you have been speaking to each of us. We thank you for your work among us as a body as we come before you.

> We now place this night again in your love. Give us the wisdom to know where you are leading us. We want to be your people in the world of today. We trust that we can hear your voice and learn the steps you wish us to take. We want to be led by your Spirit, and not just according to our own wishes.

> We now ask for your blessing, as we come before you, through Christ our Lord. Amen.

Scripture:
Acts 2:42-47 is read. It tells about the reaction of the people in the early days of the church to the experience of Christ risen from the dead. It included meeting in the houses of one another.
After a time of silence the scripture passage is read again. People are now encouraged to tell aloud what a particular word or phrase may have meant to them.

Teaching:
The following guidelines and resources will be helpful:

1. 'Where two or three meet in my name, I am there with them' (Mt 18:20).

2. *Christifideles Laici* tells us that the Holy Spirit continues

to renew the youth of the church and that this is witnessed in many ways, among them being 'the flourishing of groups associations and spiritual movements' (Par 2).

3. 'So that all parishes may be truly communities of Christians, local ecclesial authorities ought to foster the following: (a) adaptation of parish structures according to the full flexibility granted by canon law, especially in promoting participation by the lay faithful in pastoral responsibilities, (b) small, basic or so-called 'living' communities, where the faithful can communicate the Word of God and express it in service and love to one another; these communities are true expressions of ecclesial communion and centres of evangelisation, in communion with their pastors' (CL Par 26).

4. 'Ecclesial basic communities, which come together within the church so that they may be closely united with her and contribute to her development, will be nurseries of evangelisation and will be of great service to larger communities especially to individual churches. As we said at the close of the synod, they will be a source of hope for the universal church' (EN, 58).

5. 'Any pastoral strategy that omitted small christian communities would be creating a church without a future': Bishop Jode Stileto of Mozambique at an East African Conference of Bishops, which was reflected in the final documents.

6. 'A solitary Christian is not a Christian.' Tertullian.

7. 'Parishes need to restructure because parishes as we now have them are ineffective': Arthur Baranowski in his book, Creating Small Church Communities. In his parish in the USA there had been 250 people participating in 24 small groups. The parish plan he worked towards was that eventually all parishioners would attend such a group.

8. Throughout the world, especially in South America and

in Africa we see a phenomenal growth in the number of people meeting in small clusters. They have come into being with differing emphases and for varying purposes. They are also called by different names. In Brazil it is estimated that there are 100,000 small basic ecclesial communities. In Seoul, Korea up to 1,000,000 people in 100,000 small evangelistic groups meet under Pastor Paul Yonggi Cho.

9. 'The Church of the future will be one built from below by basic communities.' Karl Rahner.

10. It is becoming increasingly obvious that in the uncertainty of today's world, Sunday Mass is no longer enough if we wish to have God as a real and personal influence in our lives. In the past the culture, for all its failures, reminded us of God and his ways. Life revolved around the church. The parish hall was a centre of activity where people went to their first dance, dramas and concerts. The parish football team was often trained by the local priest. For all its weaknesses, the family rosary worked. It was family prayer. It was a reminder of God present in the home. Today we again need to discover for ourselves helps and supports to encourage us to live a Christian way of living. As far back as 1976 Pope Paul VI declared to leaders in Charismatic Renewal in Rome that 'one either lives one's faith with conviction, enthusiasm and joy or that faith dies'. That too seems to be a choice that each of us has to make, to find our own helps to live a vibrant faith or we too will 'walk away'. For many, meeting as groups of friends with the purpose of taking a greater responsibility for their faith is providing the inspiration and the help they need.

11. In 1990, 28 people at Ballinteer in the Dublin suburbs, after a course similar to the one you are undertaking, formed 4 small groups, which they called cells. During the last 7 years more than 250 other people of almost all age groups joined them, to form at one time 31 groups. Almost

all those who initially participated continue to be active. The experience has had an immense influence upon each individual and upon the parish. The initial impact was that here was a place of belonging within the church – a place where a person was known and recognised, and welcomed for their own sake.

Hearing of the common search for a deeper faith in God, and in particular hearing the prayer and the scriptural reflection of a fellow parishioner, had a big impact upon people. Knowing that there was a place where people could talk openly about seeking a deeper faith and relationship with God was an answer to a deeply felt need. It was great, too, to have a place where one could go to and seek the prayer of others at a particularly difficult time. People shared a concern to pass on faith to others, most especially to family members. Now here was a forum where they could listen to the faltering efforts of others to share faith and in this way be encouraged to seek God's help in this area for themselves. From the teachings and from listening to one another they also learned new approaches and techniques, which were of great benefit to them in introducing the question of a personal faith in some of their relationships. As people began to put into words a brief prayer, a personal reflection on the scripture, or an attempt to share faith, they realised they had something to give. Their confidence about articulating their faith grew rapidly. It seemed as if all they had heard about the faith became alive for them and with it a readiness to speak to others about what they had always considered to be private. It was in giving that they received most. The cells truly became nurseries of evangelisation. This explains in large part their rapid growth throughout the parish. More important, what was experienced was a greater trust in God's active presence in one's life and a greater facility in prayer and in reading scripture as the Word of God.

12. Format of Meeting:

The following is a general outline of the structure of a cell meeting
   20 mins: Song, prayer, scripture reading.
   20 mins: Sharing of the week's experiences: Prayer and evangelisation efforts.
   10 mins: Teaching.
   15-20 mins: Discussion on teaching – understanding it and its application.
   10-15 mins: Intercessory and healing prayer.
   10 mins: Fellowship.

13. Steve Clarke, in *Building Christian Community* (Ave Maria Press), wrote about the importance of establishing a 'counter culture' to the prevailing secular ethos of the world. He claimed that the fidelity of Christians was being eroded by values hostile to the gospel. Despite our best efforts, our faith is weakened by the value system of the world around us. Hence to live with any degree of Christian enthusiasm, we need to find supports that will help us to be in contact with the Christian story. Each of us needs to discover what is most helpful for ourselves. Preferably, it is best to be part of a people where we can see the gospel being lived. The old adage holds much truth: 'Faith is caught not taught'.

NB: An alternative way to present this meeting would be to invite people from an existing Cell Community to speak of its impact upon individuals and upon the parish. Those listening would then hear at first-hand a living experience.

Questions:
   1. What has been the one lesson that you learned from the course (briefly)?
   2. (a) How do you see your faith, and the spirit of the course, being supported by you during the weeks ahead?
   (b) How do you see the cell experience applying in your situation?

*These questions are again dealt with in the small groups. It is
important to be inviting people to make personal responses to
the questions asked. There is a brief time of feedback.*

Conclusion:
1. It is important to take up some aspects of the feedback
given for analysis and to draw practical conclusions.
People may undertake very different commitments. Some
may even think that what they are already doing is sufficient. This time is one of facilitation, leading people to clarify and to make decisions that will best help each to find
support and to live their faith. It is important that the follow-up be clear. You may consider a flipchart helpful.

2. The experience to date suggests that many will want to
continue to meet, either by way of finding out more about
small faith groups or to take deliberate steps towards organising themselves to meet in such a group. Undertaking
the formation of faith groups will take on its own momen-
tum and the leader, with the core team, can have confidence that the Lord will direct them to offer the correct
suggestions and decisions with clarity and vision at this
final night.

3. Thank people for their generosity and their example
throughout their attendance at the series of talks.

Final Prayer:
  Lord Jesus, we thank you for the power and the influence of your Holy Spirit, who is ever at work
  leading us into all the truth. We thank you that during these weeks we recognise the movement of your
  Spirit in our lives and among your people. You have
  drawn us into a deeper understanding of our own
  dignity as called by you to be your people today. We
  thank you for the clearer understanding of who we
  are as people on mission, being your presence and
  your voice among the people we meet.

We thank you for all who have served us during these weeks, who have inspired and challenged us through their words and example to play our part in the mission of the church.

We thank you for the example of the early church. It gives us a vision of who you want us to become – a people at worship together, and meeting in our homes to share our understanding of you with one another, rejoicing together in prayer, learning together at your feet and sharing your goodness to us with one another.

We entrust our hopes and our lives to you. We trust in the wisdom and guidance of your Spirit to lead us to decisions which will draw us closer to you. We pray for courage to live out our commitments. We pray for the gift of joy, knowing that you call us to be co-operators with you as 'you make all things new'. We pray for the gift of love for all whom we meet.

We make our prayer through Christ our Lord. Amen.

Sing a hymn to conclude the evening.

Fellowship:
It is always a good idea to end with a cup of tea or even with a reception to which each one has brought something to eat or drink.

Follow-up:

Where the course has led to a deepening of faith and where those participating have caught a vision that they can make a difference through sharing faith, you can assume that a majority will wish to explore further the possibility of cell groups. You may adopt one or more of the following suggestions:

1. Invite all to a supper night. Be imaginative. Make it different. Cheese and wine. Have a participant share the sense of new beginning that grew for him/her during the course. Let another 'dream' about what is possible through small groups in the parish. Facilitate the formation of a few cell groups, selecting homes and choosing leaders with details about the time, place and duration of training.

2. The Veritas video: 'A New Vision of Parish Renewal' may be shown during the week after the course, followed by a discussion and arrangements for further plans.

3. Fr Michael Hurley and the Ballinteer Cell Community will be only too happy to share with you at any time and to arrange to make their personnel and resources available to you at your request.

4. You may decide to bring all those interested to sit in at the cell meetings nearest to you. This has always proved most successful.

5. The Ballinteer Community will be happy to make available to you outlines of the Leadership Formation Courses and other courses as well as communicate the strategies of evangelisation that they have seen work.

6. Get as many people as you can to pray for your community that it may become a place where everyone is a witness and an evangeliser, and where help is available for all to live their faith with enthusiasm, courage and joy.

PART II

Cell Groups

CHAPTER 3

Introducing Cell Groups

Towards the beginning of the Lenten course, we heard rumours of a phenomenon that was taking place in the parish of St Boniface in Florida, where more than five hundred people were meeting weekly in small faith-sharing groups. This attracted our attention because courses so often come to an abrupt ending – the final night arrives, with the inevitable 'goodbyes' in spite of the often-expressed wish to continue together. Only for a few will it lead to some form of ministry or involvement in a faith meeting. Could St Boniface provide us with a format, making a follow-up possible?

Our enquiries led us to Milan. In mid-June 1990, the parish of St Eustorgio hosted an European Workshop on the Parish Cell System of Evangelisation. I, with three fellow parishioners, decided to attend. We travelled, largely at our own expense, to see at first hand the suitability of the cell experience to our own local situation. We arrived late at night. The huge church of St Eustorgio stood drearily near the city centre, its environs a meeting place for drug addicts and people of the night. It was cold and damp. We thought we had come to the wrong place.

All seemed so different the next morning as a hundred and twenty people from throughout Europe were warmly greeted by the cell community at St Eustorgio. The music was enthusiastic, the talks inspiring, even though after four intensive days our ears buzzed from listening to the translations in the earphones. While much of what we witnessed was cultural, it proved to be a most impressive event. The enthusiasm and spirit of commitment was evident. We were witnessing the joy of new converts. The service rendered to all the guests, the prayer base, with adoration of the eucharist being especially encouraged, the sense of community, and the ideal of evangelisation left a deep impression upon each of us. We spent many hours, days and even months discerning the application of what we had witnessed to our faith-sharing groups. We reported back to them. There was an enthusiastic welcome. The cell groups were launched. A central characteristic would be a clear commitment to evangelisation. During the first three years, they grew very rapidly in number as people invited their friends and neighbours. What was most evident was how people grew in confidence in their relationships with God. They learned a sense of their own goodness as unique before him, with their own special contribution to offer.

A History of the Cell Experience:

In the 1980s, Irish-born Fr Mike Eivers worked as parish priest in St Boniface, Florida. He knew that the American church was going through, at best, a holding operation. As he prayed for direction in his own ministry, in part prompted by illness due to overwork, he observed that there were churches which were vibrant and active, and where growth and mission were strong features. None of them were Catholic. They were largely Pentecostal. This led him to take a closer look at them and to determine their reasons for growth. As part of his analysis, he visited Korea to meet with Paul Yonggi Cho, who today pastors a cell community of about 1,000,000.

He drew a number of conclusions about these growing churches:

a) Each individual had experienced a renewal of faith through the outpouring of the Holy Spirit as at Pentecost. Their faith was expectant of God's intervention.

b) They met in large assemblies. Worship was joyful and alive. All participated.

c) What was of even greater significance was that they also met in small house units. This enabled fellowship and friendship to be fostered. People knew they were welcomed. They were pastored and encouraged. It was an ideal place for a dialogue of faith where their questions were heard and where they learned to express their faith in sharing and in prayer.

d) Prayer, the use of scripture, and the availability of teaching were important.

e) There was a strong commitment to evangelism, to going out to the market place to share faith.

f) The involvement of so many in providing leadership and in ministry was remarkable. Indeed all were active in ministry in one way or another. The pastor was influential in teaching and in providing vision.

The conviction of faith, the growth, the clarity of mission and the degree of participation stood in sharp contrast to the uncertainty, the dwindling congregations, the inward looking analysis, the politics and the passivity that was the mark of so much of the American Catholic Church as he knew it. After much reflection and prayer, and after seeking the discernment and wisdom of many, the parish cell system of evangelisation, adapted to the Catholic culture and drawing from the riches of its tradition, was born. After some teething difficulties, cell groups began to form rapidly throughout the parish. At one time up to 550 participated in these groups. Instead of these adding to his work load, his burden of responsibility to provide pastoral care for every parishioner lessened. Once he had provided training and ongoing supervision, he knew he had many co-workers. He claimed that, of all the initiatives he had ever undertaken, this yielded most fruit.

This attracted the attention of many who were seeking

approaches to building parish communities which, above all, would be reaching out to the lapsed and alienated. Many parishes adapted what they witnessed in St Boniface's to suit local situations. Don Pigi Perini, parish priest in San Eustorgio, Milan, visited Florida with ten of his parishioners. Today about 1,000 participate in 100 cell groups in San Eustorgio. This has in turn been a catalyst for parishes throughout Europe to adopt cell groups as their pastoral plan. This is particularly true of parishes in Italy and in France. At one time more than 300 were active in 31 cell groups throughout Ballinteer. Ballinteer, together with such diverse places as Carrickfergus, Co Antrim, St Michael's and St Agnes's, Belfast, Nenagh, Callan, Co Kilkenny, are pioneering the cell system as a strategy of evangelisation in Ireland.

A feature of this strategy is that there is no limit to the numbers who can be involved. Moreover, a large number of cell groups does not add greatly to the workload of the leader responsible. Rather he is energised in knowing that there are people who love him and support him. They simply look to him to make available to them the gift of priesthood as a spiritual leader. Pastoral care is provided within each cell. People receive help and support in a small group setting. Hence the importance of selecting people with the gift of leadership and supporting them through a leadership course and regular meetings. This has indeed been my experience. Once the hard work of the first six months had been completed and a good base formed, it involved little effort on my part. Rather it was a source of great consolation for me to know that were the entire parish staff to be away from the parish on holidays, the work of pastoral care and evangelisation was ongoing.

CHAPTER 4

What is a Cell Group about?

Communities of cell groups arise as pastoral initiatives by individuals or by a few people who seek to be church in a particular locality. They can be understood as a particular movement of the Spirit or as a specific pastoral response to the teaching of the church, seeking to speak to contemporary culture.

The stated purposes of a cell group are sevenfold:
1. To grow in intimacy with the Lord.
2. To grow in love of one another.
3. To share Jesus with others.
4. To serve within the community.
5. To give and receive support.
6. To raise up new leaders.
7. To deepen our Catholic identity.

A cell group is described in the Leader's Manual from St Boniface as 'an *Oikos*-related, multiplying small group that seeks to evangelise, disciple, and shepherd through daily relationships'. It is the interaction of four to twelve people in a group setting, knowing that 'where two or three meet in my name, I shall be there with them' (Mt 18:20). Cell meetings normally take place in a private home. Where the development of cell groups has been adopted as a parish pastoral plan, they exist to offer each parishioner a prayer experience and to help them to share faith. The ideal is that everyone is an evangeliser.

Being *Oikos*-related is central to the cell concept. *Oikos* is

the Greek word for household or a house of people. It is
often used in scripture to refer to one's extended family. It
suggests those with whom we are in daily contact, those in
the home, in the neighbourhood, in the places of work and
leisure, in the school and in the shopping malls. This is our
area of missionary activity. We don't need to go elsewhere
to evangelise – we evangelise as we go. Opportunities to
share faith surround us each day. It may be as little as saying to someone in difficulty that s/he will be remembered
in our prayer, or helping a child to understand the religious programme. It may simply be to encourage another
to pray about a particular situation. On occasion there will
be more evangelistic moments when one shares one's personal faith story and where one may even lead another in
prayer for a deeper awakening of God's love. Moments to
encourage faith present themselves to everyone. The cell
groups exists to help people to be alert to such moments,
to train people to be sensitive and respectful in sharing
with another, and to support them to have the courage to
speak when it is correct to do so.

The cell group is not the important entity. Rather it exists for each individual. One's faith may be perceived as
weak or strong, but each person has an equal mandate
from the church to witness and to share faith with others.
This is in our teaching, as for example in *Evangelii
Nuntiandi* by Pope Paul VI and *Redemptoris Missio* by Pope
John Paul II. It is our understanding of the meaning of the
sacraments of baptism and confirmation. Evangelisation
does not come easily and naturally. We often leave it to
others to do. We have understood missionary activity as
what happens in third world countries. It comes more easily to us to see faith as *private* and not only as *personal*.

The cell group exists to help people towards sharing
faith in a confident and sensitive way within the network
of their relationships. The cell is about each individual
availing of such help. Hence there is practically no emphasis

on *membership* but rather on *being fellow pilgrims*, each seeking help and inspiration.

Part of the format of each cell meeting is time given to a review of moments of witness since the cell last met. This has proved to be the most difficult part. Faith, like the air we breath, has surrounded us during life, and we take it for granted. It is often difficult to recognise and to put into words what we have taken for granted. Yet, generally, faith plays a bigger part in people's lives than is first presumed. The time of review sharpens one's focus on the actual place one gives to God. There is also a greater wish to pass on faith, especially to one's children, than is at first thought. The review makes one alert to the everyday possibilities for sharing faith and helps one to adopt a vocabulary and an approach in making the most of those possibilities. These moments are best understood as divine appointments, as moments of the Holy Spirit. One is not alone. The Holy Spirit is the Evangeliser.

The examples shared during the time of review will normally be very ordinary. They will tell of the very stuff of life in relating to another and of some word of faith spoken. During this time people also seek the advice and prayer of others in order to know how to react to a particular situation and speak faith within it. It is often appropriate too to share failure and lack of courage. We do not wish to run the risk of appearing as weak, silly, fanatical or vague before another. Hence the cell meeting provides an option of bringing these fears before God and others for discernment and advice. This part of a meeting can be one of great celebration, when one has risked the sharing of faith or undertaken something different. Pat is an elderly gentleman. He loved his wife and kids. He searched for a bible in the house when he began to attend a cell meeting. He failed to find one. There was great rejoicing when he informed all that he had gone into town that day to buy a pocket bible.

Oikos evangelisation is grounded on the conviction that God looks to people to make him known and that the normal way of achieving this is by using the ordinary relationships of our lives. Every life is complex, at least at times. In our own life and in the lives of those of our *oikos*, there are constantly evolving situations. People of anger and pain, those dealing with loss – the death of a loved one, a broken relationship, redundancy – those suffering from addiction and illness, cross our paths each day. We are not to be selective in our loving, nor in seeking to point those we meet towards the good news of faith. The idea of *oikos* evangelisation is that we have a responsibility towards those we meet. It is love in action. It is to share faith with another as the expression of our love. We may often share faith with people who will never attend a cell meeting. Some may never even know of their existence. But for the evangeliser the small group remains as a support and a place of learning and inspiration.

Programmes to involve again those who are lapsed and alienated from the church are becoming available. The experience of *oikos* evangelisation in Ballinteer is that many who have been distanced from the church have entered a deeper faith. They now enjoy the fellowship of sharing in the life of a faith community. All this is done in an informal and friendly atmosphere and adapted to the needs and questionings of the other.

Cell participation also provides a process of aftercare. The person who has come to a deeper faith can now journey with fellow pilgrims. The one who is experiencing difficulty is assured of the prayer and support of others. This is possible where the person is receptive. In times of resistance to hearing of faith, the person is loved and served. This is not a time for sharing faith, which can easily only further alienate.

Sharing of faith and an invitation to a cell meeting are distinct. The primary motivation is love, which on occasion will mean the encouragement to a deeper trust in God's goodness and providence. Each person regularly brings those of their *oikos* before God in prayer. They seek wisdom as to their needs, and as to what loving them means in their concrete situations. For some this will mean an invitation to participate in a cell meeting as a support to faith. In turn they will realise that, as a baptismal privilege and duty, they too are called to witness.

Oikos evangelisation is never easy. We have long established patterns of relating with others. The introduction of a faith content will strike us as a great risk, because we are bringing another element into the way we relate. It may seem that this will change the relationship or that the other may not understand. This in fact does not often happen. Normally another appreciates the genuine effort to help.

At times it does bring some unease. This easily works itself out if the relationship has been a good one at the outset. It is important that the one sharing is at home with their faith story and that their motivation is love. There then emerges a better and deeper relationship. Bernadette had that experience. Her best friend from school days was Geraldine. When she told her of her new found interest in her faith, it meant a strain in relating. They began to meet less often. There was an air of uncertainty. This lasted for about six months until Geraldine asked her to pray for a particular difficulty that had come up for her. Today their relationship is deeper and more honest that previously. This is very apparent in the case of married couples, who often say that the quality of their family life and the way they now relate is so much better and more open.

Oikos evangelisation is obviously adaptable to all cultural backgrounds. It is not a ready-made programme, nor a detailed worked-out plan. It is the relating of friends, taking on their imagery, language and expressions. It is a one-to-one and a like-to-like sharing. Each person has their own distinctive way of telling their story and of adapting it to the other.

A cell meeting reflects those who attend. Each cell is a community of diversity, with people of different ages, interests and commitment. Their common bond is their awareness that each is called by God and wishes to be a witness according to the gifts he has given to them. The worship, reflections on scripture, the teaching, sharings and prayer emerge from the faith, understanding and needs of those present. In fact a cell is adapted to the last person who attends. A new person changes the meeting. The 'success' of a particular meeting is not judged by how people have felt, but rather how well people have been served, especially the last person. The overall prayer and purpose of a cell meeting is determined by the evangelistic needs of a particular area. It is to be a leaven in a community. Hence *oikos* evangelisation is ideally suited to diverse backgrounds and has the capacity through the influence of individuals to bring a proclamation of the gospel to all areas of social life.

Cell people take *oikos* evangelisation seriously, not just because it is scriptural and in church teaching, but above all because it is love in action. Evangelisation is not manipulation, even though people are most open to a deeper faith at times of crisis and major change; nor is it indoctrination. Mother Teresa describes it as having the love of Jesus in one's heart and sharing it with others. It thus becomes the story of one beggar telling another beggar where good food is to be found. This explains why often during the time of intercession, someone will offer a prayer of gratitude for the one who invited him/her to a cell meeting. In 1985 George Gallup carried out a major study in America. He found that the 12% who described themselves as committed Christians were happier, healthier and more integrated as individuals and in their relationships than the rest of the population. He also discovered that the lifestyle and attitudes of the nominal Christians were no different from those who professed no religious beliefs. Authentic love will seek to share with the extended family about all that leads them to a happier way of life. *Oikos* evangelisation seeks to serve and help another. It is listening. It is spending time. It is caring. It is being available. It is holistic. Within that context of loving and serving it is also sharing the hope that is within us and the word which brings life. Amid the ordinary events of everyday it is being alert to offer a faith perspective.

Multiplication

Multiplication is another central concept in the cell system. In fact, this is where it gets its name. Growth is through the multiplication of cells. This idea is a constant reminder that the cell group does not exist only for those who attend but that its primary purpose is evangelisation. Multiplication is the great test of an outward looking attitude and a barometer of the spirit of evangelism.

Multiplication is the formation of two new cells from the parent one, when about twelve participate. It allows for the participation of more people. It is never an easy step to take. People have been together for a period of time and it has enriched them. They have encountered a deeper faith and have shared a common vision of announcing good news. They have enjoyed each other's company, have laughed together and have shared some of each other's burdens. Naturally they would wish to continue together. It is precisely at this stage that it is right to multiply. They have experienced the good news of being church, of prayer and fellowship. They now know that the gospel news works. They now have another story to tell. They are eager to invite others to share in a fellowship that communicates life.

The timing of multiplication is important. To do so too quickly would mean that the rich experience that develops within the cell may not have been shared. New cells then would start impoverished. There needs to be a healthy in-

teraction in fellowship, an attitude of evangelism and a
sense of God present among them. To delay too long is to
run the risk of a group beginning to look inwards and become over comfortable. This also means that newcomers
will find it more difficult to enter into its life.

The Format of a typical cell meeting
20 mins: Prayer, song and scripture reflection.
A candle is lit to open the meeting. There follows a brief
prayer, which may be spontaneous. Two or three hymns
are prayerfully sung. The same scripture is read at each
cell. After a time of silence it is read a second time. There is
then the option of sharing personal responses.

*20 mins: Sharing of week's experiences: Prayer and evangelistic
efforts.*
This is a most important part of the meeting. In some circles this may be called a review of life. The emphasis is on
efforts in sharing faith. Initially it is difficult and there is
the temptation to move on quickly. We can be slow to
recognise our own efforts and reluctant to speak about
them when we do. It quickly becomes central to the meeting. It becomes a time of bonding. It is not always about
'success' stories. When someone speaks about not knowing what to say in a particular situation, this invites the
prayer of others.

10 mins: Teaching.
This is a talk on tape. This can seem daunting. It did for
me. The first number of times I spoke on tape I found it so
artificial. I missed the human reactions. It seemed 'cold' to
me. My moment of 'conversion' was when I got very encouraging feedback. I then realised I was being listened to
by people who wanted to know their faith and proclaim it
in the market-place. There is usually some link with the
scripture. The tape is best when it is inspirational as well
as informational.

15-20 mins: Discussion on teaching – understanding it and its application.
Two questions are set to evoke personal responses and comments.

10 -15 mins: Intercessory and healing prayer.
This is a time of prayer for the parish, for world issues, for those of the *oikos*, for family members, etc. Usually all express a prayer during this time. The second part gives those present the option of stating a personal need. All then take a few moments in prayer.

10 mins: Fellowship.
A cup of tea, a few biscuits and a good chat.

Confidentiality must be agreed upon within each cell.

The above structure is a general guideline. It is important for a sense of purpose, order and discipline. A focus, like a candle, is encouraged at cell meetings. Each action may be led by different members of the cell, for example:
One person leads song and prayer.
One person leads the sharing on the week's efforts and experiences.
One person leads discussion on teaching.

CHAPTER 5

The Inspiration for Cell Groups

A cell community looks to four sources for its motivation and inspiration. Firstly, it takes as its model the figures in the scriptures whose lifestyles were evangelistic. It looks closely at the way Jesus related to the different categories of people he met. The way he trained and formed the twelve, which we could say was his cell. He then had a different relationship with his other disciples. 'The Lord appointed seventy-two others and sent them out ahead of him, in pairs, to all the towns and places he himself was to visit' (Lk 10:1). Often the crowds came around him to hear him teach and to be healed of their infirmities. The motto of the cell community can be summed up in the great commission he gave to his followers:

> 'Go, therefore, make disciples of all the nations; baptise them in the name of the Father and of the Son and of the Holy Spirit, and teach them to observe all the commands I gave' (Mt 28:19-20).

> 'Go out to the whole world: proclaim the Good News to all creation' and 'while they, going out, preached everywhere, the Lord working with them and confirming the word by the signs that accompanied it' (Mk 16:16, 20).

The second great resource is the teaching of the church, in particular, *Evangelii Nuntiandi* by Pope Paul VI and *Redemptoris Missio* and *Christifideles Laici* by Pope John Paul II. These have become, in effect, the text books. They communicate a great vision of the church as missionary. They are also helpful in that a sentence or a thought from one of them can at times be the basis of a teaching. Many cell participants have dipped into them.

The third factor of motivation is the actual world situation today. The cell groups critique and analyse current social and cultural trends and see in what ways faith can speak into them. They also take up Pope Paul VI's judgement, 'Many people who have been baptised live lives entirely divorced from Christianity'(*EN*, 52) to discern how the reality of a personal God can best be communicated. These are not distant trends and issues but for many are of real concern within their own family.

The fourth inspiration is what is understood as the practice of the early church. I will deal with this in greater detail as we tend to give less attention to it than to the other sources.

The Early Church

A number of features and attitudes become clear as we read about the early days of the church.

The church seemed to be the only society that did not exist for the sake of its members. It existed for the benefit of those who were *outside* its ranks. Its entire life was organised so that it could give its message and its life away. It was all directed so that others would hear the good news and be invited to share in its life. This motivation came from their own personal encounter with Jesus, and from recalling his life and words: 'Go out to the whole world, proclaim the good news to all creation' (Mk 16:16). People were sent out from the community to establish local groups and churches, which were often small in number. At times they did not spend a lot of time in these places. Their emphasis was to train leaders, who then rather quickly had to take on responsibility and preside over the new community. These leaders then had to rely upon the encouragement and teaching of travelling teachers and upon letters from the founding apostles. Acts 13:1-3 is particularly interesting. The church at Antioch, after a prompting of the Holy Spirit, and after prayer and fasting, laid their hands on Barnabas and Saul and 'sent them off' to proclaim the gospel and to gather together communities of disciples in different places. Leadership was always a team ministry. Barnabas and Saul were sent forth together. The church at Antioch had five on its leadership team. They comprised people of different gifts. The gift of prophecy – the ability to apply God's word to practical situations – is mentioned as is the gift of teaching, the grace of being able to draw from the scriptures to lead others deeper into the mystery of faith.

We often hear the debate as to how to balance the tension of looking inwards upon the community and outwards towards the world. It is the question of how to hold in balance a strong life of the community, through time spent together in developing personal relationships at leisure, reflection, courses and seminars, and on the other side, total availability for the purposes of evangelisation. It seems that in the early church everything was geared towards sharing its good news. There was only one goal: evangelisation. Every meeting, every relationship and every activity was directed towards this. 'Father, may they be one in us ... so that the world may believe it was you who sent me' (Jn 17:21). Their unity together was to be a parable of faith for others. Indeed, many internal tensions and difficulties evaporate as people commit themselves to mission, which then gives way to a more living spirituality and healthier relationships.

There was little place for the 'lone ranger'. Evangelisation was the *raison d'être* of the community. It was not the sole responsibility of any one individual. All were concerned that the gospel be preached to the ends of the earth. It was their very thinking. It was the reason, as they saw it, why they were called into existence. It was the community which sent people out and supported them through prayer and fasting. They were never sent out alone. They went with another or with a team. This working together as a community explains in great part the rapid spread of the Christian message.

A second feature of the early church was that people met in their homes. We see many examples of this in the Acts of the Apostles and also in the literature of the first two centuries. It was home. It was the natural and informal place for telling stories. It was easy here to relate the influence of Jesus in your life, to read and to reflect together on the scriptures, to pray for individuals in their specific needs, to join in song and in praise of God, and to explore together ways to reach out with faith. In the home it is easy to move from worship to fellowship, to addressing specific needs of those present, to celebration, to prayer and scripture.

It is interesting to note that in practically every place around the world where there is great growth in accepting the Christian message, small groups meeting in people's homes are a central feature. Some people fear that division and a break away from the church will occur where small groups are adopted as a strategy of evangelisation. This fear has no basis where leaders have been carefully selected and where proper training has been given to them. In fact, where people have experienced the reality of church in the home, they more easily and more naturally see their Christian commitment in terms of the church.

A third aspect that is noteworthy is that the emphasis on evangelisation was not on inviting people to an event or to a crusade, but rather on going out to where people actually met. People were going out to the wells, the places of recreation, the fields and to any place where people were living and meeting. This turns much of our thinking on its head. We more easily assume that were we to come across the right programme, or the right preacher, we would be able to gather everyone together. *Their* thinking was to go into the setting where people lived and worked, and there proclaim the message of Christ in a way that the hearers would understand.

At times this meant sharing with and challenging a small gathering of people at the street corner, in the field or on the shore of the lake. At other times it involved a personal conversation with an individual in one's family or neighbourhood. It meant giving time in a one-to-one setting, leading another to a deeper faith commitment or in many instances to a personal relationship with Christ through question and answer, the giving of information, the sharing of one's own story, or through introduction to one's own house gathering. Various recent studies in the United States conclude that on average 85% of people who have lapsed and who return to a deeper faith, do so at the invitation of a friend or family member.

A fourth feature was the personal dedication that motivated people. It was God's love that pushed them on. They were secure in his love of them. 'It is for this I struggle wearily on, helped only by his power driving me irresistibly' (Col 1:29). There was passion in their proclamation because each had been changed and enriched through their encounter with Christ. They lived with great hope and confidence, because they expected God's Spirit to guide them as to what they should say and do. They expected him too to demonstrate with power and divine interventions the truth of what they preached. 'Lord take note of their threats and help your servants to proclaim your message with all boldness, by stretching out your hand to heal and to work miracles and marvels through the name of your holy servant Jesus. As they prayed, the house where they were assembled rocked; they were all filled with the Holy Spirit and began to proclaim the word of God boldly'(Acts 4:30-31). 'The Lord supported all they said about his gift of grace, allowing signs and wonders to be performed by them' (Acts 14:3). This expectation and personal commitment meant that they were prepared to face criticism, hatred, animosity and even death with joy, considering it an honour to suffer for the name of Christ.

The First Recorded Cell Network

We find it in Exodus 18:13-27. Moses was being over-worked. He had responsibility for so many. They brought all their issues and concerns to him. They brought their disputes for him to pass sentences of right and wrong. He had to work a long day from morning to evening. Moses did not think too much about this. People were coming to him. They needed him. He had no escape. He was busy. He could not even have a day off. He was good at his job. He settled many disputes and taught people about the statutes of God. Jetro, his father-in-law, was observing all this. He knew the work was too much for him. He did not wish him to suffer burn-out. He feared that his daughter might shortly be without her husband. So he presented a plan to Moses. He must change things. He was to see himself as representing the people and their disputes before God. He was to be their teacher, telling them about the law and what God expected of them. He was to call them to responsibility. He then was to chose leaders and appoint them over groups of 'thousands, hundreds, fifties, and tens'. These leaders were to be capable and God-fearing, trustworthy and incorruptible. They were to work with the groups, care for the individuals and settle their disputes. They would refer only the more difficult issues to Moses.

Jetro assured Moses that God would be with him and would bless this undertaking. 'If you do this you will be able to stand the strain, and all these people will go home satisfied' (v 23). Moses took his father-in-law's advice. The leaders cared for the people. Moses prayed and taught the people and dealt with only the bigger issues. God blessed this new departure. People were more satisfied that ever. Moses had more time for himself and for what was important. He established a system of pastoral care through small groups. He no longer had to attempt the impossible in caring for so many. He had set up a system of evangelisation, where leaders took responsibility in discerning what God wanted in situations as they arose. No doubt the leaders also helped those in each group to care for one another and to speak about the statutes, when together and with strangers.

CHAPTER 6

The Fruit of the Cell Experience

The advent of anything new will always raise questions. The introduction of a cell system will be no different. Each parish has its own history and its own procedures and ways of decision-making. Individuals view parish life from the perspective of diverse theologies and spiritualities and have found their own 'corner', often in some tension with those who hold different views. The cell system may appear as just another change. It will mean the involvement of people not previously active in the parish. This will act as a threat to some, even where they continue active in exactly the same way as before. They fear a diminution of power and control. Also, it is not possible to explain in a few sentences what is essentially an experience and a process. All this, then, calls for great sensitivity.

Change follows a predictable pattern. It evokes a resistance. This is the attempt to keep what is perceived as new at a distance and not to disturb the comfort zone. There follows a tolerance, a recognition that there is much that is good in what is proposed, even where it does not lead to one's involvement. Then may come acceptance, that here is something that is good and beneficial. Often there may follow assimilation, becoming very involved and proposing what is new as one's own idea. Where cell groups are promoted, no doubt some of the same responses will be evident. This time of uncertainty will be fruitful when it is approached with an understanding of the psychology of change, with good preparation and planning and with pa-

101

tience in giving those with criticisms and misrepresenta-
tions time and a listening ear.

Priests at times may be reluctant to adopt the formation
of cell groups. They can see that now they will need to relate in a more personal and even vulnerable way with people. This, they claim, has not been their training and often
not their style. They fear that control will be wrested from
them by parishioners who are informed and who operate
from a living faith. It is ironic that we can look for a laity to
share in the mission of the church and often resent them
when they present themselves. A helpful point of reference for all here is St Paul's image of the body and its
many parts working together for the kingdom of God. It is
precisely in the working together of gifts that the body of
Christ forms and develops.

The perceived large workload that cell groups will involve may also deter parish clergy. There is some truth in
this, at least in the initial stages. However, this difficulty
quickly evaporates. It becomes a joy to work with those
who are receptive and eager to hear the Christian story. It
is inspirational to witness the readiness of lay brothers and
sisters to commit themselves to God and to the parish
community. It encourages one's own faith journey to hear
those of fellow parishioners. It becomes a source of gratitude to see the results in individuals and throughout the
parish as a community. Where cell groups are vibrant a
number of features emerge.

Cell groups bring the scriptures down from the shelves
of the biblical scholars to the sittingrooms of the people.
There are examples of people who did not even own a
bible purchasing one and now finding in it the voice of
God.

A time of daily prayer is encouraged. There is normally
an awakening of the sense of God in one's life. Prayer,
then, changes from the saying of prayers to using them as
a help to relate to God as person and as friend. Where peo-

ple had previously been too busy to pray, most now take a daily time in intimacy and in praise to be with the God who heals and guides.

The home as the domestic church takes on a new meaning and significance. People who may not feel too comfortable in a church building often find their way to a cell meeting. Here, in an informal setting, they discover a way of becoming church, which is experienced in the greeting, prayer, sharing, dialogue and companionship. The home becomes a prayer centre. It also becomes a school of evangelisation, from which people are encouraged and helped to go and share their faith in the wider community. This in turn makes them more likely to appreciate the church, at the level of parish, as the followers of Jesus coming to worship together, and to encounter him and one another through the sacraments.

A new appreciation of the priest develops. People look to him to make available the wisdom of the tradition of the church. They certainly don't expect him to be perfect or to be inspirational every time he speaks or celebrates a sacrament. They simply look to him to recognise them in their struggles, to share with them something of his struggle and of his faith, and to 'keep' them within the richness of the tradition. Where this happens a delightful appreciation of, and support for, the priest is evident. He too realises that he is surrounded by many co-workers in the service of the parish.

Cell groups are committed to the formation of centres of prayer and of evangelisation throughout the parish. Pope Paul VI has called such groups 'a source of hope for the universal church' (*EN*, 58). We live at a time when family prayer and a community way of life are being left behind. Experiencing prayer and reflection with others is an encouragement to re-introduce prayer in a family setting. The testimony of so many is that they rediscover the community of the parish as they seek to serve and allow themselves to be served within their *oikos*.

A new leaven exists within the parish. People are forming relationships. Bonds are being deepened. People are enjoying the friendship and fellowship of one another. What makes this different is that it is seen as the living out of the gospel. It is understood as the formation of church, as the place where people seek to be in fellowship with one another. They seek to grow in appreciation and tolerance of different personalities and viewpoints. This is the reality of each cell group. What people experience, they wish to share with the wider parish community. Hence parishioners will often speak of a deepening spirit of community. They will receive the friendly greeting, the nod of recognition and the time to be listened to. Building a spirit of community becomes the concern of all. There are then appropriate times when explicit words of faith are exchanged. A parish is transformed as more and more people take an active responsibility for the quality of loving and of a living faith within it.

Possibly the most obvious feature is the readiness of people to be involved. They become more at home with expressing the gift of faith. They take responsibility for this gift and most will seek ways that best suit them to nurture it. Many attend personal development courses, scripture classes, prayer groups, and even diploma courses in adult education, pastoral ministry and theology. All this in turn enriches their participation in the cell meeting. What is received is integrated with a view to sharing it with others. Hence, parishes where cell groups exist can expect volunteers coming forward to serve as readers, lead faith groups, train faith friends, form visitation teams, run liturgies for children, engage in social activities and recommend creative ways of reaching others with the good news. Here is a great reservoir of energy and giftedness, eager not just to undertake the 'doing' of activities, but more importantly wishing to share in the mission of the church.

CHAPTER 7

Questions and Answers

Why the emphasis on evangelisation?

The church exists to look beyond itself. It is to be a leaven. It has as its essential function the task of bringing the good news to all people (*EN*, 8). To be part of the church is to be missionary. It can be attractive to think that not every one has the gift of being a witness to God, that it is the task of just a select few. It is true there is a special ministry of evangelisation. At the same time all are called to witness. The church in its teaching turns so much of our thinking on its head. People can easily assume that concern for faith begins and ends with oneself and one's children, that one has only the task of keeping the faith. But the church challenges us to give our faith away. And that this is our essential function.

It is natural for the one who has a good news story to share it with others. Yet when we come to the story of our personal faith, there is a great reluctance to declare it before another. We prefer not to be seen as people of religious conviction. It is as if we have the greatest secret society in the world, holding as secret and private our faith in Jesus Christ. Is this because we do not experience faith as good news?

Church teaching is clear. It explains that evangelisation is more necessary to-day than ever due to religious uncertainty, loss of trust in God, moral confusion and social unrest. There is a void in the heart of people, especially of the young, which may easily be filled with syringes, fantasy and strange coloured pills, if not with the Christian story.

What is evangelisation?

Evangelisation is not a word with which Catholics are as yet perfectly at home. In their thinking it is more readily associated with tele-evangelists, fundamentalism, emotionalism, giant crusades, hard sell and aggressive approaches. Yet, it remains 'the special grace and vocation of the church. It is her essential function' (*EN*, 24). In effect we cease to be church when we lose a missionary commitment. Pope Paul VI calls evangelisation a 'complex process' (*EN*, 24).

He goes on to describe the many and varied elements that make up this process. It is a coming to know Christ as the foundation, the centre and the apex of its dynamic power. It is inspired by, and directed to, a relationship with Christ that is personal. It is preaching and sharing Christ with others and living the life of a disciple. It is participating in the life of the community, sharing the Christian life with others disciples. It involves a conversion of heart, with the person making a decision to follow Christ. It is to work towards social change.

I understand evangelisation as the expression of faith with a view to encouraging another to take a step closer to God, and to advance the reign of God. While different people place emphasis on different aspects of the process, the important thing is that each one brings their own unique gifts and insights to the job, knowing that they are incomplete. For the cell groups, stress is placed on the example of one's life. The person is to be one of integrity and truth in the workplace. There is particular stress placed on sharing the hope that comes from God. I sense that, apart from the scriptural mandate, the reason for this may be very simply that there are members in every extended family who are alienated from the church.

Is a priest necessary for this course?

No, he is not. The course can be put into the hands of a

layperson, who can run it in his/her own home. The group can then continue as a cell. An individual or a team can undertake it in an available hall. Cell groups may emerge. However, our experience to date is that where it has developed, the group had available to them the support of the local clergy. In most of the groups throughout Ireland a priest is part of a leadership team, but not always the central figure. Generally his authority is that of teacher. His concern is to make the tapes available and to empower others to work as a team. The priest is to relate according to his own leadership style, whether this be from the front or quietly supportive. His concern is always to call and train others into ministry.

Collaboration enriches all involved. Priests are often protected from bad decisions through the comments and advice that they hear at planning meetings. They have at times been 'converted' through hearing the prayer and reflections of others and thereby knowing of their commitment and love of God and of the church. It has greatly enriched them when, in their honesty, they admit they don't know all the answers and need help and advice, and when they realise that others love them.

Lay brothers and sisters have greatly benefited. They move from seeing the parish as a service station for them, where they were passive spectators, to taking on a new sense of responsibility as their calling and contribution within the community. Witnessing the priest's search for meaning and his desire for the kingdom of God gives them a deep insight into his place as spiritual leader within the community. More than ever, they will welcome him and invite him to place this gift at their service.

What do people expect from the priest?
That he be with them. That he is on their side. That he is prepared to journey with them and encourage them through their failures and mistakes. That he believes in

them. I have seen so many examples where people give so much power to the priest. We, as priests, are not always aware of this. They, healthily or otherwise, look to us for approval and direction. They need our 'blessing'. Our response is to accept this reality and create a positive climate wherein they can test the gifts and ministries God may have given them. In an atmosphere of partnership, they joyfully offer their prayer, ideas, imagination and time in the service of God and of his people.

A parish community is a set of complex relationships. It brings together diverse personalities, age groups, gifts, styles of expression of faith, vocations, etc. Yet there is order. Humourously stated, the purpose of Holy Orders is to create an order that is holy, where God is reflected from among the chaos. The pastoral care of the parish is entrusted to a parish priest, whose priesthood 'differs essentially and not only in degree' from that of others (*LG*, 10). The place of the pastor is very clearly set out in the church's vision. He exercises his ministry from within the community and not as one standing apart from it. He is its president amid its many gifts and moods, entering into its very heart to raise, as a community, its moments of resurrection and of death to God. He is teacher and healer, through living and preaching the faith in its entirety, through sacramental celebrations and through prayer for and with his people. He is facilitator in all that develops community. He is pastor and shepherd, among his people.

The concept of control, of it being 'my parish', of a 'messiah complex, it's all depending on me', has no place. Where this still exists it only keeps alive the perception of the church as medieval, with attitudes and procedures belonging to former times, but out of date in contemporary thought and operations. The church's understanding of itself today calls for a review of all parish structures to encourage and develop the participation of all as equal partners in its life and mission. It envisions small communities within the parish, where the word of God is shared, where love of one another is real, and which then become training centres to effect the work of evangelisation (*CL*, 26).

The priest has a particular concern for, and a key role in, creating a 'climate', whereby this vision begins to move towards reality. The experience is that where this climate does not exist, very good services may be provided but they remain the priest's work, with little sense of ownership by the parish community. This often leads to much frustration as the vision of the church becomes more and more widely available in courses, talks. magazines and seminars. They serve as a mirror for people to hold up to their experience of parish life. On the other hand, there can be great joy in discovering the gifts of one another and in participating together in a common mission. This is the understanding of the church that is held out to all its people:

'Priests must discover with faith, recognise with joy, and foster with diligence the many and varied charismatic gifts of the laity, whether those be of a humble or more exalted kind' (*Life of Priests*, 9).

Even in the best of climates there will indeed be tensions and difficulties as a new vision is being adopted. It calls for a new mindset, a new way of thinking and a new way of being church. There is to be great clarity about the place of the priest as one who lives by, and whose life is a proclamation of, the word of God 'in season and out of season'. He is not alone. He is surrounded by collaborators. Here is more than a new term that has found its way into religious jargon. It is a declaration that respecting the dignity and giftedness of others will motivate one's parish relationships. It is a listening to the prompting of the Holy Spirit in the life and words of each. It is seeing in another, not a threat, but a gift. It is recognising partners in the life and mission of the parish. Collaboration, then, is a way of relat-

ing and of being with others, with all the openness, participation, planning and dreaming together that it implies. It
also involves the ability to deal with issues and tensions
that arise, rather than ignoring them, or resorting to blam-
ing others.

What are the fears unique to the priest?

The path of collaboration is not easy. It challenges histori-
cal roles which were precise, clear and carried definite
expectations. They were roles which served us well in the
past. Today there are new needs and a new vision – partnership. It raises new questions for the priest and he may
fear that he will no longer have the same 'control'.

Any form of community living can appear terrifying. It
is where one enters into relationships. It is the meeting
place with others. It is to run the risk of being exposed, of
seeing one's own limitations, darkness and what Jean
Vanier calls one's 'monsters' being revealed. It is easier to
stand apart with one's negativity, criticism and misplaced
judgements. It is cosier too to interpret the life of faith as
private, concerned only with devotions and the heroic efforts to live the law. This is to miss the richness of the
church.

What happens when a priest is transferred?

This question can carry a number of nuances. It can mean
why should a priest initiate something like cell groups
when he knows he will be transferred. This line of thinking can lead to one not getting involved in anything in the
parish.

When I was transferred, I had the advantage of being
six years involved. It is difficult, a time of real grief. A new
relationship with the parish is to be established. Gone is
what people perceived as a link with the local community.
It gives rise to much uncertainty. The Ballinteer community
realised that this last year was about survival. In doing so

they discovered resources within themselves that they did not know they had. It meant that many took on an even greater initiative. They surprised themselves in how well they did.

I had always believed that the test of the 'success' of the cell groups would be seen after my departure. Then I would really know whether it was linked to a personality. I also believed that where good formation and empowerment of others had taken place in a real way, it would only really develop after my departure. I am assured that this is in fact what is happening.

There is one apprehension I have when a priest is transferred. I always stressed that an individual is a parishioner first and a cell member second. This works where there are good relationships. When there has been a happy experience of cells and of parish I fear that his transfer may have the effect of distancing them in disillusionment from the parish should doors with the parish be seen to close. They may easily become cell people first.

Priests who had been part of cell groups have been transferred to others parishes. In one case a parish priest moved after one year's existence of the cells. They gradually disappeared. They seemed to have moved from looking outwards to emphasising support. People with great needs began to attend. The groups did not have the expertise to handle them. Problems began to emerge.

Is it of the church?

What do we mean by 'church'? If we mean the local parish, it ought to be. Its purpose it to be a parish-based initiative. If we mean in line with the church's teaching, I choose two quotations from among many to speak for themselves:

> 'So that all parishes may be truly communities of Christians, local ecclesial authorities ought to foster the following: a) adaptation of parish structures according to the full flexibility granted by canon law,

especially in promoting participation by the lay faithful in pastoral responsibilities; b) small basic or so-called 'living' communities, where the faithful can communicate the Word of God and express it in service and love to one another; these communities are true expressions of ecclesial communion and centres of evangelisation, in communion with their pastors' (*CL*, 26).

'We wish to affirm once more that the essential mission of the church is to evangelise all people. It is a task and mission which the great and fundamental changes of contemporary society make all the more urgent. Evangelisation is the special grace and vocation of the church. It is her essential function. The church exists to preach the gospel, that is to preach and teach the word of God' (*EN*, 14).

Does it give rise to elitism?

The *Oxford Dictionary* defines 'elite' as 'the pick of, the best, troop or class'. There never has been any hint that to participate in a cell group makes one the best. It is seen primarily as one spirituality, one way of being church, one way of making a contribution, among many. Clearly, then, it does not lead to elitism.

To attend a cell meeting is to avail of help in living one's Christian life. It is to seek to be a better person. It is to obtain training and encouragement to break a private perspective on faith and to let it be an influence in all one's encounters. It seeks to help people to know their own faith story so as to be enabled to share it with others when it is appropriate to do so.

The only risk of elitism, as I see it, could emerge where those involved perceive the parish staff or the church as in opposition to them. This would have the effect of pushing them to rely upon themselves and their own resources. A closed inward-looking attitude, motivated by an instinct to survive, can easily develop. It is a small step to seeing themselves as those with the answers while others are wrong. A 'them' and 'us' mentality can become deeply ingrained. Where the parish staff are perceived to be supportive all such problems are easily prevented and, should they arise, are easily healed.

How do you prevent a two-tier parish?

This question could easily be rephrased as: How can different charisms and gifts be collaborated to ensure an unified church with a common missionary vision?

Canon Law places a responsibility upon those who seek 'to devote themselves... to initiatives for evangelisation, works of piety or charity and those which animate the temporal order with the Christian spirit' (*Canon* 298.1). They are to meet together and develop a programme in pursuance of those initiatives.

Coming together for these purposes may well cause some difficulty and uncertainty for a particular parish. It may not as yet possess the ability to integrate such groupings. Sr Eileen Delaney, in 'The Adequacy of Oikos Evangelism in St John the Evangelist Parish, Ballinteer, in Ecclesiogenesis', calls for an new understanding and an accommodation on both sides. She encourages a re-imagining of church. She calls for a new model of parish: 'The documents of the church since Vatican II indicate that the communal model of church is a necessity if the church is to be faithful to its mission.' She continues: 'With an emphasis on *koinonia, diakonia, kerygma,* and liturgy, cell evangelisation is inclusive of all Christ's faithful, but points to the need for a model of church that is equally inclusive.' Her particular conclusion is that without a parish vision that strives for communion and without a style of leadership that seeks to bring this about, a great opportunity to impact culture will be lost. Instead we run the risk of many good services being provided and many groupings active, but all working along parallel lines.

Will there be a loss of control for the priest and the parish team?
People are often afraid of the life of the Holy Spirit. It is a handing over of control. It is allowing for the unexpected to occur. It is creating space for mystery, for what is beyond one's control and for what cannot be explained in human terms. The Spirit changes the laws of humanity. Not everything then will be observable, explainable and controllable. It expects creativity, imagination and the unexpected. That is the nature of the life of the Holy Spirit. Scripture speaks about a 'being born again'. It is like a re-entry into life, seeing it charged with mystery, and expectant of the interventions and guidance and 'coincidences' of the Spirit.

And this creates problems where control and administration have been the motivating forces. It is easier to remain in the safety of the sea shore than to launch into uncharted waters. Where faith is not a daily living encounter with God, it is attractive to seek the security that comes from correct protocol, from a 'peace at any price' attitude, and from activity and organisation as the source of one's importance before self and others. Where this continues, the work of the Spirit as witnessed in others is often interpreted as a nuisance, as transient, and as a thorn in one's side. The result, not deliberately, is misunderstanding and hurt on all sides. The voice of the Spirit is thereby silenced, while the wisdom of Gamaliel's criterion of discernment is forgotten: 'If this enterprise, this movement of theirs, is of human origin it will break up of its own accord, but if it does in fact come from God you will not only be unable to destroy them, but you might find yourselves fighting against God' (Acts 5:39).

It is also perceived as safer not to draw too much attention to the power and gifting of the Holy Spirit. He invites us to relate in a different way with people. It will mean seeing them as equal members of the community, each with their own unique gift and service to render. It is easier to make people the objects of pastoral concern, where we relate from the basis of possessing something to give, than to share ministry with them, relating as mutually interdependent. The latter would involve listening, where the word of criticism may be a prophetic voice. It is to become vulnerable, aware that one has not all the gifts but is only a small part of the body of Christ, dependent on the gifts of others. It is to rejoice that others possess gifts and abilities that we do not have, and to celebrate when we see them being put at the service of the kingdom. The activity of the Spirit is often messy, where incompleteness and the unexpected are normal realities.

Is there a danger of small groups going their own way?

Yes, when those in leadership are in conflict with the parish mission statement and are operating out of their own hurt feelings towards the parish and the church.

No, when the parish is seen to be supportive of them and when leaders have an understanding of the mission of the church and an appreciation of the need to work collaboratively with all parish agencies.

Do home groups raise suspicions?

Another way to put this question would be: What are the reactions of neighbours to the fact that others meet in their homes? I don't know. It possibly ranges across the entire spectrum from a great sense of comfort that people pray together in the neighbourhood to uncertainty as to what new cult is being introduced. I know that often neighbours ask for their intentions to be included. I am sure such meetings raise questions and debate.

How can one have deep convictions and remain tolerant?

This to me is a most important question. It refers to the way we communicate an experience. We all know people who, in their enthusiasm, alienate others with their constant talk and insistence that they have discovered all the answers. It makes us feel inferior. We want to walk away. At its extreme religious fanaticism has had a violent history.

A number of attitudes are fundamental within the cell groups. They are seen as *one way* to be church. There is no effort to teach another. There is simply the telling of one's own story. The freedom of another is respected. Even before a story is relayed, permission is asked of the others along the following lines: 'May I tell you something of what has happened to me?' or 'May I tell you something that is important for me?' Evangelisation is understood as an act of love. Within a relationship where there is trust and respect, it points to where a deeper love and meaning are found.

Who is the Spirit?

Pope John XXIII, at the beginning of Vatican II, did not pray for 'a new theology', nor for 'a new commission'. He prayed for 'a new Pentecost'. He prayed that the very soul and heart of the church be enflamed into a new fire. He prayed that there be a new outpouring of the Holy Spirit, so that the powerful presence, and fresh breeze, of the Holy Spirit would again be evident in the church, with the same life and manifestations as at its beginnings. Pope Paul VI continued this prayer and drew attention to the need for the new life of the Spirit:

> 'The church needs her perennial Pentecost: she needs fire in her heart, words on her lips, prophecy in her outlook ... This is what the church needs, she needs the Holy Spirit. The Holy Spirit in us, in each of us and in all of us together, in us who are the church' (General Audience, 30 November 1972).

Pope John Paul II has continued to place the same emphasis on the necessity for the life and the power which the
Holy Spirit inspires and breaths in the church, without
whom it is empty. In his first encyclical he states:

> 'The time of the church began at the moment when
> the promises and predictions that so explicitly refer
> to the Counsellor, the Spirit of truth, began to be ful-
> filled in complete power and clarity upon the
> Apostles, thus determining the birth of the church'
> (*Encyclical on Holy Spirit*, 25).

For the early church, the Holy Spirit was an experience,
before becoming a doctrine. Jesus promised his followers
that he would send the Spirit, who would do things in
them and among them that they would know and observe
in their experience. They would 'be clothed with power
from on high' (Lk 24:29). He said that they would 'receive
power when the Holy Spirit comes on you, and then you
will be my witnesses to the ends of the earth' (Acts 1:8).
'The Advocate, the Holy Spirit, will teach you everything
and remind you of all I have said to you' (Jn 14.:26). They
were to receive all they would need to live fruitful lives.
They could expect wisdom. Above all they were to expect
an energy and a power beyond themselves. The Acts of the
Apostles, really the Acts of the Spirit, is a record of this influence and power at work in individuals and in the community.

The Spirit of God is not reserved for the early church.
There is not to be a watered down twentieth-century ver-
sion. It is he who gives life, who inspires communion, ministry and gifts. Without it the church is empty, a set of beliefs, a structure, a tradition. It is he who makes the church,
and makes her to be distinctive.

How will friends react?

In a wide variety of ways. Generally it is with admiration.

People of conviction are normally respected. At the other extreme, it is with suspicion and a concern whether there is a losing touch with reality. As far as I can assess, the reaction is that after a little uncertainty as to what the other may be getting involved in, there develops a greater openness to talk about the issues in life that concern them and where God may be in them.

I often recall the findings of a Gallup poll which stated that most people who get very involved in religious activity in the States lose contact with their former friends within two years. This was for me a sobering finding. I am always aware of it. It explains in part why cell meetings take place fortnightly and why each is encouraged to participate in a wide range of activities.

Are Cell Groups the way forward?

It is unrealistic to expect that any single initiative is *the* way forward. That is to expect too much from it. That is to give it an unhealthy significance. It is I believe, however, a work of the Spirit among many others. Almost everyone I have met who has participated for a period testifies to the great difference it has made for them. They have a sense of mission that is built into their everyday lives. It puts within the reach of people aspects of Christian living that are so often encouraged and written about today, in particular that faith is to impact one's life, that the Spirit of God is active among his people, and that small faith groups have a vital part to play. I sense, too, that evangelisation, with its many faces, will be far more urgent in the years ahead. The formation of cell groups is exciting for a parish.

Does the parish change?

Putting evangelisation on top of the agenda as diocese, parishes, individuals and groups, challenges us to a totally new mindset. It pushes us to look creatively for new ways to proclaim the gospel in a rapidly changing culture. It

makes us review the expenditure of effort, time and resources in terms of how effective they are in leading others
to a new and deeper living faith.

The impact upon the parish is immense. When people
are in relationship with God and are looking outwards,
they will be seeking informal opportunities throughout
the parish to encourage others to a deeper faith. They will
also seek new and imaginative ways to present the gospel.
You will also have available in the parish people who will
readily take on very diverse services, from church cleaning
to proclamation of the word of God as readers.

What about young people?

In Ballinteer more than sixty young adults participated for
about four years. Today, while there are far fewer, all will
speak about the friendships formed and the influence that
these years had upon them. The spontaneous and informal
setting of the cells, with their emphasis on fellowship,
knowing God's love, and entering into conversation with
others, seems to have been ideal for them. In fact many
gave extra time to form teams who travelled widely meeting other young adults and sharing with them their presentation of the faith in mime, dance and song. The cell
format and emphasis was adapted to their stage in life.
Then college, emigration, boy/girl/friends began to take
its toll on numbers attending. Possibly the greatest difficulty is attracting young people in the first place.

Canon John Hogan and Sr Patricia O'Donovan had a
novel idea in Nenagh. They facilitated meetings for four to
six nights each school term for youth. They considered ongoing commitment as too much for young adults. They
place great emphasis on friendship.

Will people be disappointed when you raise their expectations?

We will all have our own fears as we undertake something
new. This was one of mine. When I witnessed in Milan the

possibilities of the cell groups for parish renewal, I was struck by the fact that to begin on such a journey with people would mean that I could no longer hide. I knew I could easily gather people together. I knew I could communicate the enthusiasm I witnessed at Milan. But what would I have to offer after a few months? Expectations would be raised. They would look to me as leader. I was looking about six years ahead and I could see people seeking something new.

On our return we immediately sought the advice of Canon Sean Carey. We then visited Bishop Donal Murray, our area bishop. I voiced my concern. His advice meant so much to me: that to look that far ahead is never to undertake anything.

Is it a movement?

No. I see it simply as an initiative being adopted by many parishes to offer people the experience of a deeper faith and of community. Knowing good news, they are then encouraged to share it.

Do people join? Is there a membership?

The answer is no to both questions. It is an offer being presented in a parish where those who wish can avail of a faith support network. It is understood that it is the Spirit of God who evokes responses in the hearts of people. It is at his timing that people participate. There is freedom to continue attending or not. The decisions that others make are seen as part of their sacredness. When someone ceases to attend, we believe it is important to say goodbye and thank them for what they have offered to the group. We have learned that this is more delicate than it appears. I remember one person interpreting this as a subtle pressure to return, which genuinely was not intended.

Where does social justice come in?

Not directly as publicly expressed. It becomes part of the way people relate to one another. There are examples from Ballinteer and elsewhere where self-employed had no work. They were supported through the voluntary contribution of others. Those who could not afford an anniversary celebration were surprised by a large party. In times of hospitalisation and illness, there is a ready stream of support. There is ongoing prayer for those in need. Many have been trained in counselling skills so as to offer a beneficial ear to the uncertain.

Are cell groups cultural?

At National Seminars this is a question that is always asked. It goes something like this: 'It works in Ballinteer which is middle-class, where people are articulate and have easy access to books, etc., but what about the poorer places?' The answer is in two parts. Cell groups have taken root in a wide variety of settings, from rural to urban, from the upper to the lower classes. Secondly, it is not a programme to be followed. It is about friends coming together to pray and chat together as a support in living out their faith. The language, the interaction of people, the teaching, the praying is readily adaptable to those involved. In fact the emphasis on evangelisation as relational means that to be effective it will be adapted to how one friend relates to another. The middle-class have their strengths. The greater strength of others is that there often is a greater spirit of community and openness to one another.

Bibliography

The following are some of the books which I have found helpful and which I would recommend as further reading:

The Adequacy of Oikos Evangelisation in St John the Evangelist Parish, Ballinteer to Ecclesiogenesis, *Sr Eileen Delaney*, (MA thesis, All Hallows College, Dublin)
Building Christian Community, *Steve Clarke*
Cell Leaders' Training Manual, *St Boniface's Parish, Florida*
The Contagious Congregation, *George G. Hunter*
Creating Small Church Communities, *Arthur Baranowski*
Creating the Evangelizing Parish, *Frank DeSiano & Kenneth Boyack*
The Marginal Catholic, *Joseph M. Champlin*
Mustard Seeds (1985), *National Committee of Diocesan Youth Directors in Ireland*
The Parish as Learning Community, *Thomas Downs*
Parish Renewal (2 Vols), *Donal Harrington*
Partnership in Parish, *Enda Lyons*
Pass It On, *Michelle Moran*
Renewing the Catholic Parish, *Joseph Lange*
Small Christian Communities, *James O'Halloran SDB*
Take Heart, Father, *William J. Bausch*

Many of the quotations in this book are taken from transcripts of focus groups, carried out in cells and leader groups by Annette Farrell in May/June 1997.